Leadership for Success

A Dynamic Model of Influence

DR. ALFRED NKUT, M.D.

AuthorHouse™
1663 Liberty Drive
Bloomington, IN 47403
www.authorhouse.com
Phone: 1-800-839-8640

First published by AuthorHouse 2/17/2010

ISBN: 978-1-4389-6615-1 (sc)

Printed in the United States of America
Bloomington, Indiana

This book is printed on acid-free paper.

authorHOUSE®

To Lise

[signature]

To my truly amazing family, my wife, Elaine Blacklock,
and our children, Jacob and Ruthie.
Thank all of you forever for filling my heart with boundless love.

Acknowledgments

First, I would like to thank Jessica Lachance, whose company, Vertigo Design Group, helped research this book.

I must also thank Katherine Bruneau, a rising star. I admire her typing skills, organization, and invaluable insights that played a critical role in shaping Leadership for Success.

Oscar Gionet is a great emotionalist and counselor. Thank you for your insights on how to make this book better.

I express my gratitude for my in-laws, Don and Gloria Blacklock. Thanks especially to Gloria for your support, encouragement, and insights on Leadership for Success.

Dave Rowe is one of my heroes. He graciously agreed to join me in feeding the hungry as a way of relieving poverty. His insights on this noble cause that we both share an interest in has spilled into all the aspects of my life.

Emmanuel Pekum had learned how to pull up himself with his bootstraps from mediocrity to significance. He is a rising star, technocrat, and millionaire. But my deepest appreciation goes to him for the time and resources he sacrifices to care for my parents, Joseph and Susan Ndenkeh.

Special thanks to a great star, Barrister Nico Halle, who has taken up the mantle of the pioneer presidency of Equity Bank Cameroon, one of my greatest monuments.

Ann Marie O'Neill is a wise and deliberate encourager. Her illuminating insights meant a lot to Leadership for Success, and I thank her for them.

Thank you to Author House and our editor for their guidance.

I. The Paradigm Shift

When you are inspired by some great purpose, some extraordinary project, all your thoughts break their bonds: Your mind transcends limitations, your consciousness expands in every direction, and you find yourself in a new, great, and wonderful world. Dormant forces, faculties and talents become alive, and you discover yourself to be a greater person by far than you ever dreamed yourself to be.

Patanjali, the great philosopher

Chapter One

The Paradigm Shift

The Heroic Mission

You have the choice to behave in a manner worthy of being followed as a leader all the time, whether at home or the workplace. It is of great importance that the people who choose to follow you do so out of respect, not obligation or fear.

- You need a foundation of ethics as well. This is best expressed through Aristotle's classification of leadership as ethos, pathos, or logos. *Ethos* relates to ethics, the values held in common by society that defines what is good and bad. In order to be convincing to your followers, you need to be logical. *Pathos* relates to passion for your vision. Showing some emotion and excitement connects belief in your cause, and it is very inspiring for your team members. Before they will follow you, people want to know that you believe in the cause, too. *Logos* is ability to think precisely and creatively and to help others believe in what you are saying

Leading is simply the process of helping yourself or others get somewhere. This may involve changing your own thoughts in order to adopt a new paradigm. You may sometimes have to influence people to change their perceptions as well.

Leadership qualities like integrity, vision, discipline, and many more described in this book form the basis of leadership. Most of these qualities have to do with your character or who you are. Not so many of them deal with what you do. Most of leadership has to do with who we are, not what we do, even though what we do is also important in leadership. It's also because this book does not deal with positional leadership or authority. Whether you are in position of authority or not, this book is aimed at improving your life and making a difference. If you are in a position of authority, this book will help you become a better leader by the practice and acquisition of these qualities, that is, self-improvement.

The topics chosen are deemed to have the key principles that are foundational for being a good leader. I initiated a research study that the Vertigo Design Group completed to find out how one could use his or her ability to influence for success. It's long been observed, however, that most of our success comes from within. It's my conviction that most of our success comes from our inner motivation, attitude, and efforts rather than external factors. Success comes from within.

"A heroic mission is a vehicle that transcends both you and your purpose to something bigger than you. It has the quality of immortality and legacy."[1] Its essence is for the common good, thus it's both personal and universal. Ralph Waldo Emerson described it as knowing that "even one life has breathed easier because you have lived." So the scope of one's mission is irrelevant. We cannot all be generals. We need some foot soldiers, and all these roles contribute to make for success. If the foot soldier does not do his or duty with diligence, there will hardly be success at the top. Genuine or heartfelt service is the key. Just having a positive worldview is a good start. Then a good deed, no matter how small it is, is always better than none is.

The examples of quiet heroes in our world are innumerable. Don Matthew, a retired teacher, spends his time as a volunteer at a food bank and helps children who are having difficulty reading. Drs. Geoff and Eleanor Protheroe have dedicated most of their working life as physicians doing mission work in Africa. They have worked with the African Inland Mission (AIM) organization in many countries, including Kenya, helping the medically needy. Knowing what these two great doctors are doing, the inference that helping the poor is part of their heroic mission is inescapable. They are undoubtedly quiet heroes. Just like Mother Teresa, the poverty activist, they are just doing their bit to make the world a better place. After all, we are all part of the greater tapestry.

---

1   Jeffrey Sonnefeld, *Firing Back.*

The MIT professor, Peter Serge, who coined the term *heroic mission* said:

> The leader's purpose story is both personal and universal. It defines her or his life's work. It enables his efforts yet leaves an abiding humility that keeps him from taking his own success and failures too seriously. It brings a unique depth of meaning to his vision, a larger landscape upon which his personal dreams and goals stand out as landmarks on a longer journey. But what is most important, this story is essential to his ability to lead. It places his organization's purpose, its reason for being, within a context of where we're headed, where the 'we' goes beyond the organization as a vehicle for bringing learning and change into society. This is the power of the purpose story. It provides a single integrating set of ideas that gives meaning to all aspects of the leader's work. Out of this deeper story and sense of purpose or destiny, the leader develops a unique relationship to his, or her, own personal vision. He or she becomes steward of the vision.[2]

A heroic mission is like a compass. It guides you as it aligns your goals with your values. You could measure yourself against this standard of excellence day by day.

In Amos 7, we read about another kind of plumb line. The Lord first told Amos about a swarm of locusts and a great fire, which were pictures foretelling the destruction of the Northern Kingdom of Israel. After the prophet prayed and the Lord agreed to delay his judgment, Amos was given a vision of a straight wall. The Lord was standing by it with a plumb line. Because Israel's conduct did not square with God's laws, they experienced God's wrath.[3]

As followers of Jesus Christ, we have a plumb line by which we can evaluate our lives, that is, the word of God with its principles and commands when we are faced with moral choices. We must see what the Scriptures teach. When we follow the Lord's directives, we need not fear what his plumb line will reveal in our lives.

---

2   Peter M. Senge, *The Fifth Discipline: The Art and Practice of the Learning Organization.*

3   . Amos 7:8 - 9

The most important question in life has always been, "Why live?" And, again and again, the answer has been pointed to purpose. More precisely, it has been pointed to the purpose behind the purpose. This is the societal impact that your mission has. But why live if you have no purpose? As you think about it, imagine how boring life would be. There's no dog in the hunt, so life would be very flat. There is no life without the struggle. This is what fires you up and keeps you going day by day. Without a purpose or mission, life is not worth living, and there is no direction. In that way, you just waste your energy. The heroic mission harnesses your energy for an end.

In other words, your life is focused, so effort, time, and energy are not dissipated through boredom. This inspires hope for the future because you expect the best to happen. This affects the way you see life, and it determines both your journey and the destination.

Several religious and ethnic systems can help in shaping your values. My own value system is based in part on the teachings of the Christian Bible. Because Christianity is the most familiar religious value system in North America, I will use it to explain some of the principles of leadership. The Bible makes it very clear that, if you have not loved, you have neither lived nor succeeded. It says that God is love, too, and he made us to manifest his love. To love others is to love him. Also, service is the highest calling there is.

Mutual empowerment is a great law. The easiest way to move forward is by helping people reach their own potential. The barrier to such empowerment is fear of losing your own position. It's a paradox that only very secure people understand that, when you try to lift up somebody, you're eventually lifted, too. If you try to pull someone down, you lower yourself as well. Have you ever noticed that, if you smile at a perfect stranger, you will receive a smile in return? That simple act makes you feel so good. However, if you get up on the wrong side of the bed and stub your toe, then everything just seems to go downhill from there.

In that same way, by helping someone move forward, you are also helping yourself. It could be just by the good feeling you get, or it could be from the experience that you have gained by working toward the goal of helping that person reach his or her dream. The opposite also holds true as well. Though, by ignoring an opportunity to assist another person, you are ignoring the opportunity to grow yourself, missing the experience, and holding yourself back as well. The principle of abundance is crucial here. You think there is enough to go around, as opposed to scarcity mentality. Simply stated, the Law of Attraction is that you attract what you focus on. In other words, if you focus on receiving what you want to see in your life, you will attract it. But, if you focus on what you do not want in your life, that is exactly what you will attract because what you do not want as your main focus is.

Here are some of the measures of success: abundance, contentment, loving, heroism, and attainment of excellence. Success accrues as a by-product of the effort concentrated in pursuing your dreams. Once you connect to a cause and clearly decide what your life would represent, it engages your heart. You become emotionally engaged around the cause, and there will be a corresponding release of passion and energy, the buzz.

This is how you get charged up like a magnet. In my dynamic model in chapter six, I explain how you become like a dynamo, radiating hope, love, ideas, and energy rather than being flat and bored. This spills into all areas of your life, including how you think and speak. This puts a spring in your step. By the end of this book, a whole skill set, values, and character traits will be discussed that will affect your thinking and behavior.

This change in mentality leads to a paradigm shift for the better. Awareness often precedes all action. Your thoughts are so important that you cannot do anything without first changing the way you see things. Your thoughts shape your perception of a situation or the world. Thus, create a heroic mission that is not only in alignment with your values, but those of the organization and/or the public as well.

Who Am I? (Identity)

Part of the discussion in this book is modeled on more than sixty leadership qualities that the Vertigo Design Group researched. Many studies have been done that invariably put trust or vision as the top leadership quality to possess.

So the content of your mind is conditioned by the above factors, including belief systems, your childhood, culture, family background, and much more. The real issue is how you adopt an identity that is a true reflection of who you are, egoless.

Ego consists of thought and emotion or the collective identification, such as religious or political affiliation. It also contains personal identification with possessions, opinions, and values. Your ego can become a problem when you allow it to thrive on feelings of superiority, thus making you egocentric or egotistical. In most cases of egotistic behavior, the driving force behind it is the false belief stored in the subconscious mind, surfacing to distort the conscious mind's true beliefs. It is anything that directly or indirectly says you are right or better. Thus, it can play tricks on your mind in order to stay right. This could be blatant or as subtle as blaming a situation on somebody else or staying in denial.

Being right could be identifying with a mental position, a perspective, an opinion, story, or judgment. Through awareness of other people and the outside world, you can differentiate between fact and fiction. Eckhart Tolle says:

Awareness is like the light that dissolves the darkness of ego. Thus, unconscious and dysfunctional egotistic behavior can never be defeated by attacking it. Just in the same way, you do not beat the darkness away, but bring in light to make it go away.[4]

Always remember this. How far does the darkness go away when the lights are turned on? Not very far. The message is that the battle with the ego is always on. You must always be vigilant about keeping the light of awareness turned on

---

4   Eckhart Tolle, *A New Earth*.

in your mind. Becoming egoless requires a paradigm shift, moving from "me" to "we" in your mentality.

The essence of knowing the deceptive nature of ego is that you will become a better leader through knowing the pathological nature and limitations of the ego. Thus, you have to learn how to let go of identification with psychological forms. You become a magnet (so to speak) that radiates. This determines your thoughts, words, and actions. If you can recognize even occasionally that the thoughts that go through your mind do not represent the reality, then you will no longer identify with them. In that way, you will perceive with as little biased interpretation as possible.

Mrs. Gamble was a participant in a survey regarding the primary factor in successful marriages. She had just celebrated her fiftieth wedding anniversary. She had five children, one of whom she lost in a motor vehicle accident. She became so depressed and suicidal that her husband left her for six months shortly after the death of their daughter. Grief counseling turned the tide. She successfully went through the five stages of grieving. She faced the death of her daughter, with shock and denial, for a very long time. Then she suffered a nervous breakdown as she became very angry about it. Bargaining then ensued. She slipped into a severe depression. Her self-esteem was down. Her cognitive distortion became so intense that she hated her husband and filed for separation. After so many sessions with grief counseling and sharing stories with people who had common problems, the gloom lifted, and she began to see the light.

Mrs. Gamble stopped being aware of the outside world, that is, of anything other than her grief. She did not even consider the grief of her husband or additional pain she might be causing him because of her behavior. She said that, in retrospect, her state of mind or mental disposition was the problem, not her husband. She shifted blame for everything that happened to her husband.

Certainly, when you are depressed, your self-image changes. Cognitively, your mind has changed. Why? Your self-confidence drops and so does your level of optimism. You start to expect the worst rather than the best, so it reinforces the negative attitude.

Mrs. Gamble concluded that possessing qualities like strong commitment to staying together in a relationship and being a hope-giver are important, especially in tough times. This is when the link is weakest and most likely to break. She said that, even with these qualities, life could still be very daunting to live and it is hard to see how anyone could live without these traits.

Commitment and hope can convey many messages. Just the idea that you expect to succeed uplifts you and everybody around you. When you expect the worst, you garner fear and negative mental attitude, which coalesces to psychological resistance. Not only does it pull you back, it also saps your dynamism and decisiveness, the catalyst for achieving anything you want.

Many qualities come out of becoming egoless. When you recognize the fact that your thoughts, emotions, and circumstances do not represent reality, you stop being reactive and become more proactive. Rather than live in unproductive, repetitive thoughts and emotions, you use your imagination, anticipate, and visualize possibilities.

In the end, your egocentric thinking and circumstances will cloud your judgment in every situation. But to what extent? In reality, you cannot get rid of psychological forms, emotion, and thinking. Minimizing their interference in your judgment is more to the point. As you can see in Mrs. Gamble's situation, unquestionably, her depression contributed to clouding her judgment, up to the point where she chose to separate from her husband. She gave testimony to the fact that she was committed in trusting and loving her husband, but her mind was not with her. As the fog lifted, she went back to her rock-solid values of commitment, trust, and hope. This is what saved her relationship.

For self-improvement, you may need a new paradigm to take you where you want to be. Use the think-act-feel template to practice the desired quality until it becomes spontaneous or part of the fabric of who you are. This template is discussed fully in subsequent chapters.

Fulfillment of Potential

As a psychiatrist, Dr. Molly spends time interviewing scores of people each day and has seen far too many people who just stumble through life, not achieving much and not having ambition to be anything greater. They do not recognize the fact that each minute of their time is their life in miniature. It eventually adds up to make up your life. When the most important deadline comes up or is imminent, for example, when people are diagnosed with a terminal illness and they know they have a few months to live, they get very motivated to achieve their long-cherished dreams and goals. The unique thing about this deadline is that you cannot change it. Living this way is like playing a game without knowing the rules until the last minute. Even Plato and Aristotle assert the fact that life is not merely a game of chance and that basic laws do exist.

Abraham Maslow put forward one of the most famous psychological theories of human motivation in 1954. He was trying to understand why people never seem to be satisfied with what they have. We often find that we are dissatisfied with our situation and want to do something about it. When we get what we want, it does not take long before we want something else. Maslow suggested it is important to think in terms of a hierarchy of needs. We have some basic needs. If those are not satisfied, they will motivate our behavior almost completely and make it impossible for the other needs to be met. Each need that is met propels us to the next level, and only at the top is self-actualization. Maslow saw this as the ultimate achievement, reached only by a few outstanding people. It is a worthy goal to aspire to.

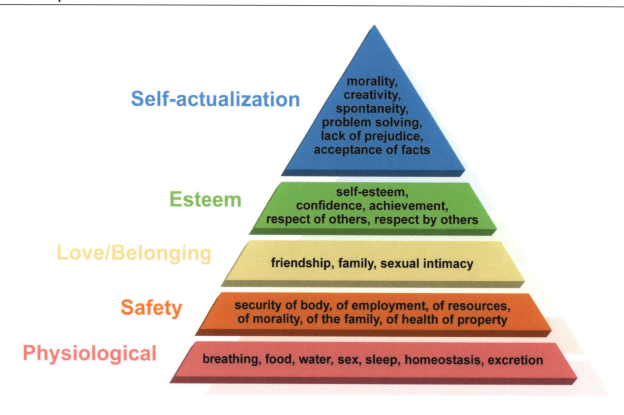

One of Dr. Molly's patients, Nimble Jack, complained of having no pep. On probing further, Dr. Molly found out that Jack watched television until midnight before going to bed. He woke up at 11:00 AM and ate lunch at noon. No exercise was scheduled into his life. This is an all too familiar story. I understand the eat-sleep-watch television lifestyle. Nimble Jack was clearly focusing on the most basic of needs in the hierarchy and not working for anything beyond. You need drive and motivation to release your potential. After spending time and working with Nimble Jack, Jack began applying himself, and he began to soar.

In order to do your best, you need leadership in any area of life, even just keeping healthy. You need to be aware of self-improvement. The small steps of getting out of bed early in the morning, exercising every day, and eating healthy are needed to consciously move you from one level to another. This is called self-improvement because this involves setting goals and discipline, which are leadership qualities. This is even more crucial in developing your gifts or finding ability in others. Leaders strive to make a difference in both themselves and in others. You make the commitment to never be less than your dreams.

To keep your momentum going, you constantly set new heights and goals to reach. This leadership spirit helps you go after your dreams and your personal best. When your mission engulfs you, excitement and passion develops. This dissolves any growing pains that tend to be associated with lack of enthusiasm.

Great leaders are not just involved with making a living. They are intent on making a life. Doing becomes a joy, not a chore. Getting out of bed early is seen as a joy, not a chore. Instilling a new habit in order to strengthen a new leadership quality is a joy, not a chore. Become an inspirational leader, one who helps people move forward. Awareness precedes action, but only constant application of a principle bears fruit. In *Master Key System*, Charles Haanel made the following observation, "The only value in any principle is in its application."[5]

A period of about one month is needed to instill a new habit. Create an affirmation regarding something you wish to experience, like a character trait in leadership. This is how you summon your desire. Shift your attention or focus to the affirmation as often as you can with the triad of think-act-feel. This is the mind principle. It remembers what you acknowledge. What is not affirmed disappears.

This book teaches you how to avoid self-imposed barriers that keep many people from living the life of abundance that they deserve. They never realize they are the ones keeping themselves behind. These people do not know the difference between primary and secondary goals. Our primary goal never changes. It is our ultimate calling. It's the purpose behind your purpose. It is the element of your mission that positively impacts the society at large. What is it for you? It is not education. It is not becoming a lawyer or a physician. These are your

---

5   Charles Haanel, *The Master Key System.*

secondary goals, mere steps on the path to achieving your primary goals. It took a lot of digging deep before I realized that a piece of paper from the university is not a primary goal in life. Nobody is born to be a doctor or hold a master's degree. We are born for a more noble purpose than that. If this is a dilemma for you, it shall be resolved by the end of this book.

Leadership goes beyond survival. It is about winning, creating significance and meaning, and positively impacting the world and creating an eternal legacy.

Dual Legacy

Dual legacy is your reward both here and hereafter. Improving the lives of other people is one way of paving the path for eternity. There is hardly any leadership quality more powerful than grace, which makes you a better servant or giver. Grace means free favor of God shown toward man. We are expected to follow this example of generosity toward other people.

In this way, we become graceful as we give or serve out of love for we expect nothing in return. When we serve with the expectation of getting something back, it is trading your service or favor. True generosity is when you believe that giving is receiving is love.

Service is the highest calling, so enjoy helping people. An attitude of serving reveals who you are. Discover your gifts and where there is need. Then go to work. You can do this by constantly reviewing your heroic mission to see if it is consistent with what God wants you to do.

Leaders visualize and see the end game. Fulfilling a legacy only on earth is a job less than half done. Recognize God's sovereignty. The more you base your identity in Christ, the more secure you will be. You can anchor your life on this unshakable rock, even in the most severe of storms. It is your holy calling, your eternal legacy or destiny. This is not an add-on because it's indispensable. This continuous process is begun on earth.

Another key aspect of love is accepting people just the way they are. Depending on how you look at it, this could be construed as forgiveness or nonjudgment.

When you simply devise a no-blame policy among the people you work with, this is very empowering for your followers. Jesus taught nonjudgment with his actions. "If any of you is without sin, let him or her be the first to throw a stone here."[6]

Nonjudgment empowers people because they can exercise their power of free will. Jesus shows you how with the story of the adulteress who was about to be stoned to death. Jesus set free every person who was about to throw stones at her or set them down out of his or her own free will. And not even one person threw a stone. Emulate Jesus' example of letting your followers exercise free will at work. In this way, you earn their respect. When you are nonjudgmental, you dramatically increase your ability to influence people to follow you, freely and willingly.

You need both worldly and eternal success. Salvation is the gateway to heaven. Believe in him in order to keep the spiritual door open. Salvation is the right path to the next world. To avoid it is to kiss darkness while forsaking the light. Worldly success without eternal success is a gimmick. You need both successes. However, even if you do not believe in God, it's difficult to deny the nobility of doing something good to benefit the world for generations after you leave it.

Levels of Growth

Self-discovery is important in self-improvement. You have to summon your desire with persistent thoughts and feelings. Hold the image long enough for the universe to manifest what you want. Only you can do this; nobody else can. Simply, someone else cannot think and feel for you. Also, you become happy only when you connect with your inner purpose, and only you know what it is. Bob Proctor observes:

[The] thermostat is our higher faculties that should change the temperature or results in the outside world. The sensory input comes in but let your thoughts

---

6   Amos 7:8–9 (NIV).

control the results. Our outside world is considered effect your thought is the cause.[7]

Studies have shown that most of the factors that move us ahead are rooted from within. Thus, most of the time, you make a situation as it is. Most of the conditions and circumstances are within your control.

Self-discovery

As we grow older, our focus changes with time. It grows. Our vision of what the world is changes with time. Just imagine how big a baby's world is. Also imagine how big your world was ten years ago. You realize, like many people I have interviewed, that the difference is like night and day. You have certainly heard the expression, "Children should be seen and not heard." These ideas and any other limiting and perceived protective notions help overtame us through our childhood. This overprotection stifles curiosity and creativity and puts a lid on the capacity to grow. These limits are lodged in the unconscious mind. Because of this, people are not even aware of the limitations put on their psychology. So you become like the elephant in the circus that is confined to a string it can break loose by using a small fraction of its strength. The elephant falsely believes it cannot do it. The elephant, just as we do, lives a restricted life, not the abundant version. All the vitality and dynamism is bottled up as potential energy or gifts that cannot be released and manifested or used.

The process of reconditioning has to occur. This has to do with unlearning some of the things that hold you back. The process of self-discovery is never-ending. We always grow. Our world gets bigger. We suffer or face crisis situations that bring us out of our comfort zone. In such times, the stakes are high. Our physiology helps, too. The adrenaline rush gets us going, and it prepares us for actions. We can jump through a barrier we never dreamed we could.

I know Jino personally. He is a tycoon in his community. His material riches are countless, but he does not live the life of abundance. He lives a restricted

---

7   Bob Proctor, The Secret to Millionaire Success

version. He lives like a pauper. He lacks sophistication and philosophical refinement.

I have observed that awareness is the single-most important factor in making a paradigm shift. You see the world as you conceive yourself to be. If you have low self-esteem, you have low expectations. The elephant in the circus is not aware of how much potential it has. Overtaming, as in very restrictive parenting, does the same thing to teenagers. As they grow into adulthood, they need reconditioning. A lot of psychological resistance holds these children back as it kills their can-do attitude. Remodeling has to happen to unlearn some of the things that have been planted in their subconscious minds. The growth process continues as well as they continue to discover who they are.

When I grew up, I always had the passion for helping people and entrepreneurialship. I still do. When I graduated from family medicine residency, I was very interested in going into the specialty of gynecology. The good Lord gave me the opportunity to go back to school to study more to become a gynecologist. I took the position and closed my family practice. I was in the program for six months. The thing that struck me most was the rat race and false glamour when you look at it from afar. My mind could wonder a lot because I did not have my family with me. I did a lot of soul-searching. I reached deep down below, where most of the treasure is buried. It only unfolds to us when we cultivate our inner space, linking it to the universal consciousness. I thought I was restricted in my family practice, but I realized I was restricted in my new specialty.

I recognized the multitude of advantages that family medicine could provide me as a career. I noticed that family medicine was very lucrative. I could set my schedule the way I wanted. I could sleep and get out of bed whenever I so pleased. I did not have to be on call in the hospital, another rat race I had been involved with in the past.

When Mother Teresa was asked about what made her tick, she simply said "finding your Calcutta" was the key for any mission. I started looking for my niche so I could exercise my gifts. I suddenly became very aware of how much more I could do, not only to create value for myself, but for the rest of the world.

I discovered that leadership was the only thing that could help me create this abundant life for others and myself. So I started the great journey of trying to know who I really was. I modeled myself according to what I believed in, my passion for business and helping people. And I was compelled to create organizations and people that could make a difference in our world. I believe in people and their necessity to perpetuate vision and influence timelessly. Nobody lives forever.

I am dedicated to starting organizations that are investment vehicles for relieving global poverty. I believe in charitable capitalism. The investment of different forms of capital in such a manner generates genuine economic growth for the poor. I started a foundation, the Nkut Foundation, for relieving global poverty. I later created Skylimit Corporation as part of the game plan for relieving poverty. Most of the money made will be used for financing poverty relief projects. Equity Bank Cameroon is part of this vision. It is also heavily involved in micro-financing as well. The goal here is to create a loop between the poor and the rich that recycles capital, enabling the poor to get into the financial mainstream.

I hope these organizations will grow and add value to people's lives. I am also dedicated to developing leaders who can magnify and carry on with the vision. By empowering those leaders, it mutually empowers me, too. In that way, legacy becomes a reality, not a myth. This is my heroic mission. You can discover yours by exploring your strengths and finding ways to use them to improve the world around you.

These are the touchstones of life. These things make people feel that you care for them. Empowering somebody to create an abundant life for himself or herself is the greatest thing you can do to a human being. It is the ultimate level of caring that I know. Once you adopt a new paradigm and create a heroic mission, you will set goals that would have blown your mind away if you did it before reading this book. You suddenly feel like a pupa that emerged from the chrysalis. You get so fired up, pumped, and juiced that you do not feel like sleeping anymore. You will feel both content and ambitious. Your perspective and attitude about life completely changes. Your faith, vision, and steps you take become bigger and bolder. You begin to feel that you merely existed before your paradigm shift.

As soon as you claim the true expression of who you are, you become the magnet that attracts what you want. Success in any form, health, contentment, prosperity, and loving are yours. Make a resolution today that others may lead small lives, but not you. You should be celebrating this anniversary as you walk the earth.

By the end of this book, you will learn how to move your attention and focus on the worthy or what you wish to experience. You will learn to be like the termites, taking little bites of action at a time. Day by day is what brings about success, not huge jumps. Not only will you learn how to set goals, you will learn how to stay focused, keep your momentum, be task-oriented, and get things done.

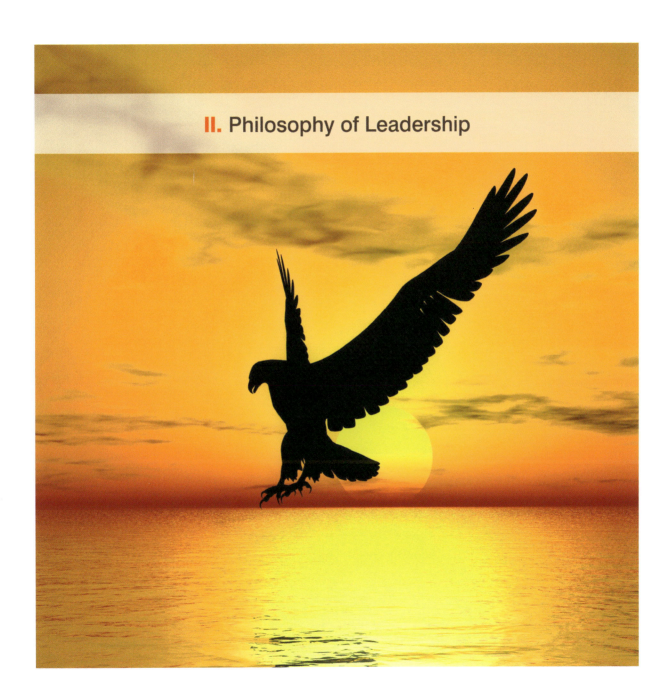

II. Philosophy of Leadership

We are all angels with one wing.

Author Unknown

Chapter Two

The Philosophy of Leadership

Impacting Your World

For most of us, our formal education does not teach us how to deal with life challenges, goal-setting, spiritual maturity, and motivation to succeed. These all have to do with self-improvement, which teaches us how to live by design, not default. Living by default is like playing a game of poker without knowing the rules. Your life would be rooted in bedrock of self-leadership, the drive to action. You will inevitably become a pragmatist rather than an ideologue as you will always ask the commonsense question of what works rather than what the books say.

When you become aware of the fact that most of your drive to succeed comes from within and life is a bumpy ride, you begin to perceive adversity differently. Your level of curiosity will grow as you become purpose-driven. But, above all, you will be changed and strengthened in a very powerful, positive, and unexpected ways. This book is like a coach. You will consciously seek out counsel for practical solutions to problems.

The big bang theory does not work in self-improvement. Leadership is not one big thing you do. It's a deliberate art. Lots of little things you do have a cumulative long-term effect on your life. So acting with intention as opposed to being reactive is a dimension of leadership. It determines who you are in terms of your attitude. When you practice measuring twice and cutting once, it makes your responses more measured and proactive. This is all leadership.

I have observed that a sense of security is your best source of psychological strength and stability. A lot of fear comes from insecurity. It puts a ceiling on how far you progress in life, your passion, and energy.

When you feel confident, you are more likely to be an active agent in your life, making your own choices and deliberately influencing what is likely to happen. Lack of confidence refuels anxiety and procrastination because you are more likely to anticipate pain rather than success in a given situation. This is all self-improvement.

Nimble Jack was determined to develop his leadership skills. He was very wise and knew he needed repeated study and practice of the leadership qualities until they became second nature. He explained to Dr. Molly how he practiced his heroic mission day and night. He sounded like a man truly on fire. He adapted my trademark of Skylimit as his mantra for his new life philosophy.

Nimble Jack was surely taking the right move to genuine growth. Dr. Molly knew that he was already functioning in level one of Bob Proctor's levels of leadership competencies. At this level, you wake up from sleep as you become aware of the fact that you have been moving backward or sitting at the same place and complaining and blaming the whole world for your seeming woes. He also knew that Nimble Jack had hit this stage when he consciously took the initiative to seek self-improvement.

It is true that you cannot go beyond your expectations, so having the knowledge provides the options to know how short you are from attaining your mark. Here are the levels of competency, courtesy of Bob Proctor, author and motivational speaker. He describes four levels of competencies that could be achieved by growth through practice:

I. **Unconscious incompetence:** You are losing. You are not doing well. You are not living in abundance. In other words, you do not believe in the infinite source for provision of all you need in all areas of your life: spiritual, emotional, physical, and financial. You think in limitations. You think like the circus elephant, in limitations. The elephant does not believe in the unlimited power of its mind in order to summon its desire and create it at will. The key hallmark to this stage is that you start to wake up from your sleep. You do not take responsibility. You blame the world for your situation.

II. **Conscious incompetence:** It is a new dawn because you start to take responsibility for what you have created, your life. You start to ask the big questions. Is this your purpose for walking the earth? There is a possibility of change of direction if you are not aligned with your inner purpose. You realize that life is slipping past you. The attitude here is that you trade things because, even when you give, you expect something in return.

III. **Conscious competence:** You take a direction consistent with inner purpose. You want to do something. You start to trust your gut feeling. You constantly affirm what you want. You are putting out, giving energy into the universe. The attitude here is that of gratitude. You genuinely give out of love; you expect nothing in return. You are in the passion zone. You are just doing it. Eventually, self-mastery and masterminding leads to the fourth stage.

IV. **Unconscious competence:** Here you sense that the source is infinite. It's coming through you, not from you. Thus, you automatically give without thinking. Giving is energy. You put out love in the universe. Abundance in all areas of your life is yours.[8]

Because the focus of leadership in this book is on personal prosperity and impacting the world, I added to the preceding four stages of leadership growth: personal value and social value. So personal value here relates to creating value for you; social value has to do with creating value for others.

Leading is about moving yourself or others somewhere. Often, it's about moving forward. In that way, your actions have to make a difference. That is, they must add value to you or others. Such a value does not have to be motivating. It may just be feeling good or a quality of sorts. Dr. Molly told Nimble Jack many times that, if any action he performed did not make a difference, then why would he bother. We set out to do anything because we at least feel or think that it will create an impact. Knowing human nature very well, it is fair to say that the solicited impact could be negative as well. But here I want you to do the things that have a positive impact for yourself and the world at large. If your action does not create a positive impact, then the effort is wasted. In that sense, you might as well buy a gun, close your eyes, and shoot a bunch of ducks in the sky.

The crux of leadership is influence. This makes position and title much less important than values and impact in leading. Also, with experience, I know that seemingly small actions can have profound effects. Shortly after the story of Hillary Clinton dodging sniper fire in Bosnia was brought into light as not true, an opinion poll was conducted in the United States. She trailed Barack Obama by 23 percent regarding integrity. Did this affect people's decision on picking Obama over her as a good choice for the Democratic presidential nominee? Of course, the court of public opinion was very clear on this one. Aristotle broke leadership down into ethos, pathos, and logos:

Ethos: Being true to yourself and your values and being authentic

- Pathos: Having empathy and passion
- Logos: The ability to think precisely and creatively and to help others believe in what you are saying

Historically, the emphasis on leadership has changed throughout the years. This has gone from the management era, where the emphasis was on ensuring productivity in others. Then came the leadership era, where creating a vision was emphasized. Leadership is more preoccupied with the why of the mission. But doing right and doing your best is also important. This is because professionalism, ethics, and results are important in leadership.

The greatest influence in the world comes from selfless spiritual leaders like Jesus, Buddha, and Mother Teresa. They have experienced spiritual awakening. In this way, they have a very contracted ego, which does not get in the way of their being or ability to be an agent for positive change. They were awakened to their primary or inner purpose, which is in alignment with their secondary or outer purpose.

Eckhart Tolle calls this "awakened doing."[9] That is when consciousness flows through you as you align inner with outer purpose. This links you to the creative power of the universe. This is how you can bring the light of consciousness to the world. It's the true path to being successful as well as experiencing joy and enthusiasm in life. With awakened doing, your goals are dynamic and a vehicle for positively impacting the world, not just a projection of your ego.

The abundance mentality is to think and feel that there is enough for everybody, that is, there is enough to go around. This is contrary to the scarcity mentality, which inspires limitations that tend to stifle progress.

Like attracts like, as in the Law of Attraction, so feelings of availability open endless possibilities. It puts you in the mood to give, and giving initials receiving from the universe. If the giving is not accompanied with the expectation of anything in return, it feels ever so nice. Giving in any form, service, or act is very fulfilling.

When you come from the mind-set that there is enough for everybody, you maintain your success with poise and without tension. It makes you learn to share your success liberally with others. Teach and inspire others how to use these practical techniques to achieve great results in their lives. In this way, you guarantee the flow of creative ideas around you.

Mutual empowerment happens when others become more prosperous and successful. It strengthens everybody. People who could pass the baton to subsequent generations emerge. This is how legacies are built as well as truly successful abundant living.

The scarcity mentality is one that is fraught with many vices. Many wars in the world have been started because of the pamper mentality. Thousands of people live desperate lives of fear, self-doubt, insecurity, and codependence out of this negative mind-set. And real lives have been lost through real wars. And families and friends have been pulled apart as well.

---

9   Eckhart Tolle, *A New Earth*.

The Spiritual Perspective

David Roper tells the story of an elderly missionary couple who served God for fifty years in a remote African village. They returned to the United States for a well-earned retirement. When they arrived, however, no one was there to greet them because of some confusion at the mission office. They had no one to help them with their suitcases and no one to move them to their new home. The old gentleman complained to his wife, "We've come home after all these years, and there is no one who cares."

The man's bitterness grew as they settled into their new home. His wife, a bit fed up with his complaining, suggested he take up the matter with God. So the man went into his bedroom and spent time in prayer. When he came out, he had a new look on his face.

His wife asked, "What happened?"

"Well," he replied, "I told God that I've come home and no one cares."

"And what did God say?" his wife asked.

"He said, 'You're not home yet.'"

You may also serve for years in a place where no one notices you or cares what you have done. But God sees and cares. One day, when we reach our eternal home, "Each one's praise will come from God."[10]

As you can see, the world rewards success, and God rewards faithfulness. If you care about God, you should care about the things he cares for. He asks us to follow his commands. He also asks us to help the needy. This great couple did just that.

A measure of spiritual maturity was lacking with this great missionary couple. Give thanks in all circumstances. Quite often, our circumstances burden us. We fail to see the big picture, but these are temporary if you stay focused. Character lasts forever, even into eternity.

---

10   Colossians 1:16.

Part of spiritual maturity is the ability to get along with your team members. A spiritually mature leader is truly humble. He thinks about others and not himself. Humility builds bridges; pride builds walls. You need this to be able to cultivate a team spirit. You need other team members in your organization or life as well.

What kind of a picture or metaphor is your life? This is critical in determining your destiny, not only on the planet, but also of the eternal realm. Biblical values and wisdom are foundational to living a life that is worthy. No book talks about human nature as the Bible does. Who said getting wisdom is the wisest thing you can do? Precepts of the Bible, like hope, wisdom, and love, are foundational to building character. Character traits are crucial for being a great leader. As a leader, you must learn how to read into situations, trends, people, and yourself.

As a leader, you will realize that sometimes going ahead with your goal may seem like swimming upstream, but the faith you have in your mission keeps you going. We are spiritual beings with a human experience.

There is hardly any better measure of a man than his values and ideals. It's very important to be principled in your quest for leadership. These are like the plumb line that gives you direction or the compass that does the same. Your belief shapes your thinking, actions, and perceptions. So what you believe in is very important.

The key to making a paradigm shift is to link yourself with the worthy. You can radiate kindness, control your tongue, and have a selfless attitude.

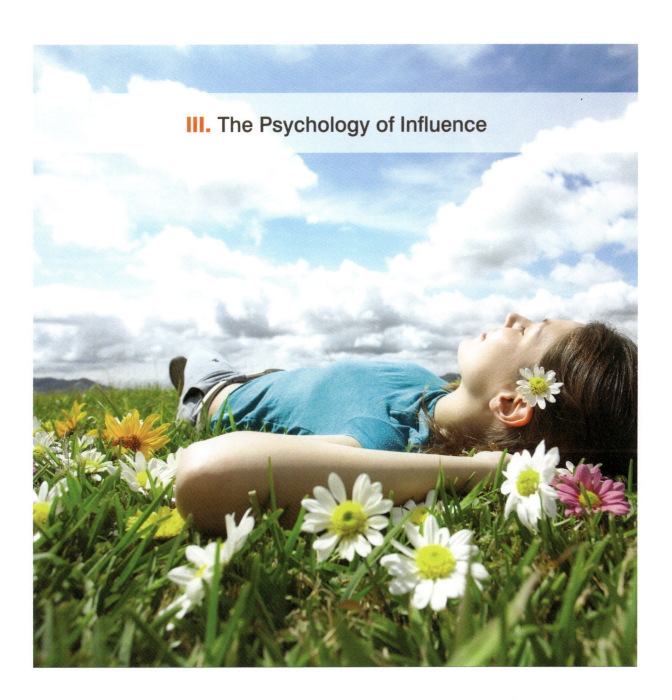

III. The Psychology of Influence

The thermostat is your higher faculty that should change the temperature or result in the outside world because these are effects. Your thoughts are the cause.

Bob Proctor

Chapter Three

The Psychology of Influence

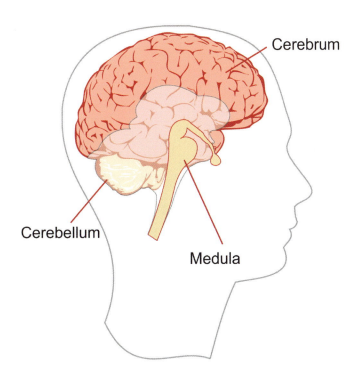

The Mind Principle

To influence people, you have to alter their thoughts, actions, or behavior. So knowing how people think and act is important. Decisions are made in the mind, either consciously or unconsciously. It is your greatest gift, so knowing how it works and how to use it is crucial. Psychology is the science of the mind that is concerned with human behavior and personalities. If you know how to use your mind, you can model most of the qualities of leadership described in this book.

Why is the mind so important? It is everybody's signature. Conscious awareness precedes most of your actions, except those that could be spontaneously mediated by your subconscious mind with very little or no thought. Awareness is important in making a change or just deciding to move forward, as in leadership. Your thoughts are the architect of your life, all that you experience, real or imagined. Your thoughts create what you call your truth or reality. So everything you are, have, or do not have is in your mind. What you think you own (for example, a house) exists first in your mind. How much value the house is to you is again in your mind.

The thoughts you harbor form your internal dialogue. This determines how you conceive or interpret the world around you. Your internal dialogue generates your external world, too. For example, when someone does not like you, it has absolutely no effect on you unless you try to hate back. Your unforgiving attitude leads to the negative emotions of hate, guilt, and regret. These negative emotions draw psychological pain or suffering into your life. Another way of expressing this is that the negative emotions choke your soul as you are chained to the past rather than living enthusiastically for today. We are spiritual and imperfect beings because we all have flaws in us. This is the rational for forgiveness. We stop resentment against someone. Like love, true forgiveness is unconditional. That is why it's the ultimate example of love. It's also self-love because it is very empowering for you. An unforgiving attitude is very poisonous for your soul. Your soul is your unconditioned self. It is really who you are. It is eternal. It is well-being or joy. It is abundant. It is perfect. On the contrary, your ego is your conditioned self. These are all the attributes, psychological or physical, that are inconsistent with the soul. Things like negative emotions are attributes of the ego. Anything that says you are lacking in one way or the other is likely the ego telling you, for example, guilt, unforgiving, and inadequacy all come from the ego. Thoughts immensely affect your chemistry, too. Having feelings or thoughts that are uplifting releases happy chemicals, like serotonin, that make you happier, too.

I like the story of a man who lived in a very remote area. He had never seen electricity before when he went to the city to visit a friend. When he saw many lightbulbs shining overhead, he concluded there were many moons in the city. At first, he thought he was losing his mind, but he gathered his courage and asked his friend, "How come you have so many moons in your city?" His friend made a joke out of him for sure, but, before he left the city, it took a lot of convincing for him to learn that it was electricity, not the moon. So, this guy could only relate with what he knew. Conscious awareness definitely precedes inspired action. No wonder that this man could have sat in a dark room without knowing that all he needed to do was turn on the switch to get some light.

The mind is your thinking faculties. Functionally, it is divided into the conscious and subconscious mind.[11] Your conscious mind is rational; the subconscious is irrational.[12] You think with your conscious mind. Whatever you habitually think sinks down into your subconscious mind, which then creates according to the nature of your thoughts. Your subconscious mind is the seat of your emotions. It is the creative mind. If you think good, good will follow. If you think evil, evil will follow. This is the way your mind works. Once the subconscious mind accepts an idea, it begins to execute it. It works for good and bad ideas alike. It uses the principle of affirmation. It upholds what you believe in. That is, it draws onto you what you think. This is why you attract all experiences in your life.

Your conscious mind is the reasoning mind. This phase of your mind makes choices. You make all of your decisions with your conscious mind, like making the choice to live in your home. Your subconscious mind, being the seat of your emotions and memories, feeds your conscious mind with the intuition based on that past conditioning that where you live now is appropriate.

On the other hand, without any conscious choice on your part, your heart is kept functioning automatically. The vital functions of all the organs in your

---

11 Cecil Andreoli, *Essentials of Medicine.*
12 Harrison Braunwald, *Manual of Medicine,* 15th ed.

body, including your breathing, are carried on by your subconscious mind through processing independent of your subconscious mind, which does not reason things out as your conscious mind does. Your subconscious mind accepts what is impressed upon it or what you consciously believe.

Positive thoughts, of course, will have an opposite effect on you. This is why the positive mental attitude is so powerful. You can reinforce this by using oppositional thinking. You will simply substitute a thought that you do not like with a desired one. You can use William James' technique to instill whatever habit you desire in three weeks.

Your mind works on the principle of belief. The belief of your mind is the thought of your mind. All of your experience and conditioning are produced by your subconscious mind in reaction to your thoughts. Thought is an incipient action. The reaction is a response from your subconscious mind that corresponds to the nature of your thought. Thus, thought is an action, and your subconscious mind reacts to it.

The belief itself, not the thing believed in, brings about the result. Stop accepting false beliefs and fears that may create turmoil in your life. When you feel anxious about an elephant under your bed, whether this assumption is true or false, you get the same reaction. The fight mechanism in your body fires up adrenaline, which gets your heart thumping fast. You begin to feel wired and sweaty, too. Thus, the belief in your own mind, not the thing believed in, brings about the result.

Your subconscious mind does not have the ability to reason like your conscious mind, so it does not dispute what it's told. If your conscious mind gives it information, right or wrong, it will accept it and act on it as true. It will bring your suggestions, even those that are false, to pass as conditions and experiences.

Everything that has happened to you happened because of thoughts impressed on your subconscious mind through belief. So repeatedly give your subconscious mind constructive, harmonious thoughts. As these are frequently repeated, your subconscious mind accepts them. In this way, you then form healthy habits of thought and life because your subconscious mind is the seat of habit.

Get your heroic mission clear and focused. You have to articulate what your end game will look like. This you have to imagine, visualize, and see the picture because only things conceived of the mind can be manifested. As Louis Pasteur observed, "Chance only favors the prepared mind."[13] When the picture is clear in your mind, the solutions and kind of team needed can then be put together. You will also be able to seize the opportunities when they present themselves.

The statistic is daunting. I have observed that most of your personal success is rooted from within. This is a direct measure of who you are. This is also the essence of self-leadership. In order to develop a worthy heroic mission, you have to understand the difference between paradigm and ego manifestations. The heroic mission is the road map or compass for the interesting journey of leadership. A paradigm is the model or approach. The invisible assumptions permeate our perceptions. They are invisible because they form the focal point of our conditioning. They shape the medium of our subconscious mind and gut feelings, and they are said to be autonomic. That is, they are fired automatically or spontaneously. The information here has already been filtered through our conscious mind throughout our life experience, dating back to as young as we can remember. These are all beliefs, values, culture, and experiences, both bad and good.

The habitual thinking of your conscious mind establishes deep patterns in your subconscious mind. If your habitual thoughts are peaceful, constructive, and free of fear and worry, your subconscious mind will respond by creating like thoughts. Hence the importance of selecting thoughts and ideas that inspire, motivate, and fill your soul with joy.

When you get in touch with your basic impulses, visualization is a spontaneous process. The decision-making process happens almost instantaneously. Intuition is commonly referred to as the *sixth sense*. This makes problem-solving psychologically complex to explain, but, in all, it simplifies the process in a practical manner. Intuition means instinctive insight into the solution

---

13   Louis Pasteur; *The Secret to Millionaire Success.*

of a problem without conscious reasoning. A decision is quickly made with little thought involved, even though so many factors have an influence on it. Instinctive behavior is more common in lower animals because their brains are not developed as in humans. The principle element in their behavior is coded in genes.

Outcomes are therefore very difficult to predict partly because multiple factors, including past experience, personality, and mental attitude, influence them.

The Affirmation Technique

To affirm is to verify the existence or truth of a thing. As you maintain this attitude of mind as true, regardless of all evidence to the contrary, you will receive an answer to your wish. Your thoughts can only affirm. For even if you deny something, you are only affirming the presence of what you deny.

Again, the conscious mind is a camera, and the power of your affirmation lies in the intelligent application or specific positives. You affirm good health with the absolute certainty that it is a virtue.

To affirm is to state that it is so. Maintain this attitude of mind as true, regardless of all evidence to the contrary in order to supplant the idea into your subconscious mind, the seat of creation. Your thought can only affirm. Even if you deny something, you are actually affirming the presence of what you deny. Keep affirming the things you believe in until you get the subconscious reaction that satisfies you.

Ralph Waldo Emerson, the great nineteenth century philosopher said, "Do the thing you are afraid to do, and the death of fear is certain." When you affirm positively that you are going to master your fears and you come to a definite decision in your conscious mind, you release the power of the subconscious, which flows according to the nature of your thoughts.

The mind principle has one mechanism, affirmation. Create affirmations based on what you know to be true and your dreams. If you hold whatever you want, positive or negative, long enough in your mind, it will manifest. This is the universal law of action and reaction. As Newton stated, the reaction is equal and opposite to the action.

Constant repetition or rehearsal is important, not only in developing a new habit, but in enhancing memory and learning as well. The brain easily remembers information when it is constantly challenged or impressed with it from time to time. The film washes away with time, and the picture becomes blurry, necessitating new impressions on the film.

The Visualization Method

The basis of this technique is the use of imagination. With constant practice, it becomes second nature, instinctive and intuitive. If the solution to the problem is not obvious, you basically toss it into your subconscious mind. Again, choices are made in the conscious mind, which is a camera. The subconscious is the film where the picture or movie is cast.

The easiest and most obvious way to formulate an idea is to visualize it, that is, to see it in your mind's eye as vividly as if it were real. You can see with your sense of vision only what already exists in the external world. The ideas and thoughts have energy and are real, so, one day, they will appear in your objective world if you truly believe in your mental image. This process of thinking forms impressions in your mind. These impressions, in turn, become manifested as facts and experiences in your life.

Oppositional Thinking

You want your attention to be on the task at hand, unless it is what you do not want to experience. The essence of this technique is to either help you stay focused or shift attention onto what you wish to experience. Simply put, if you do not like what you are experiencing, change the channel or frequency. That is, shift focus to what you want to experience. Don't try to resist what you don't like. What you resist persists. So turn on a light for darkness to disappear. Don't try to beat darkness. This is explained in chapter four, but, more broadly speaking, you can also use oppositional thinking. It is a very important technique. Simply replace the thought you do not like with one that you wish to experience.

Simply stated, you replace the thought or mental movie with one you wish to experience. Nimble Jack used this method to great effect to quit smoking. As he explained, he began to imagine the joy of freedom from the smell of smoke. He understood that his conscious mind was like a camera, so he tried to do it as effortlessly as he could. He also imagined his son saying congratulations for quitting. He focused on the scene before him until he gradually identified with the picture that had been developed in his mind. He repeated this mental movie frequently in order to have it completely impregnated. He completely believed that he would succeed. This technique had endless applications. For better healing, whatever the ailment is, imagine yourself to be free of it. See your loved ones saying congratulations and feeling good about your healing.

Beware of what you feed your mind with. If your heroic mission is filled with big and bold ideas, these will energize and motivate you. On the other hand, if your mind is fed with hopelessness and worry, this will lead to tension, anxiety, melancholia, and limitation of all kinds. When an idea comes to mind that you do not like, in order for psychological release to happen, acknowledge it and accept it. When you try to deny it, you repress it. What you resist persists.

The right thing to do is to grieve your loss. The five stages of grief are denial, anger, bargaining, depression, and acceptance. Grief could be felt over the loss of a loved one, treasured possession, or job. Again, acknowledge your true feelings about the loss. If you feel like smiling or crying, do it. They are both mechanisms of psychological release. These release mechanisms are like a valve that releases force from a pressure cooker.

So, to apply oppositional thinking, believe you can handle the situation. To effectively grieve your loss, you may sometimes need to see a counselor or go to a support group in order to share common experiences. Depending on your attitude and culture, this process may last from a few months to many years.

The essence of grieving is to once again feel at peace and centered with your life. Often, when you experience loss, it knocks you off your wheels. Just to get you acquainted with the stages of grieving so you can know what stage you are in, when you are hit with a major loss, denial and shock happens. Then comes anger and bargaining. The fourth stage is depression. At this stage, you feel down and moody. You have trouble sleeping. You lose interest. You have low energy and high anxiety. The fifth stage is acceptance. You have achieved psychological release. At this point, you are at peace with yourself. You can truly accept that you can handle the situation as it is. In the beginning, the reason you imagined that you could handle the situation was to trick yourself and create a mental movie or picture that would hasten your healing.

Habitual Mental Patterns

The analogy in the Bible is a wonderful way to understand the two functions of your mind. It says you should think of the mind as a garden. You are the gardener. You are planting seeds of thought in your subconscious mind all day long. These seeds are based on your habitual thinking so you may not even be aware. As you sow in your subconscious mind, so you shall reap in your body and the world.

Imagine your subconscious mind as a bed of rich soil that will help all kinds of seeds to sprout and grow, whether good or bad. Every thought is a cause; every condition is an effect. This is why you should take charge of your thoughts. In this way, you can bring forth only desirable conditions.

Entertain all ideas that come to mind and then release them. Do not resist these thoughts because what you resist persists.[14] This is repression, which is very detrimental to your soul and body. You can also use oppositional thinking to substitute for an idea that you do not like. Hence, substitute hate with love.

If you try to resist the word hate, it will persist in your mind. Why? Simply, the mind principle only works by affirmation. So you use your conscious mind to

---

14   Harrison Braunwald, *Manual of Medicine*, 15th ed.

choose love rather than hate because love is more consistent with your values. So affirm love, and hate disappears.

You can start right now to sow thoughts of peace, joy, goodwill, and prosperity. You can do exactly the same thing with the leadership qualities. Think quietly and with conviction on these qualities and principles. Accept them fully in your conscious reasoning mind. If you continue to plant these seeds of thought in the garden of your mind, you will reap accordingly.

Once you begin to control your thought process, you can apply the powers of your subconscious to any problem. This is the world within that creates the world without. Your thoughts, feelings, and visualized imagery are the organizing principles of your experience. The world within is the creative power. You have created everything you find in your world of expression in the inner world of your mind, whether consciously or unconsciously. If you want to change external conditions, you must change the cause, that is, the way you use your conscious mind and the thoughts and images you entertain. So, if you simply change the cause, you change the effect.

Once you master how to skillfully apply the mind principle, you will experience abundance instead of poverty, wisdom instead of ignorance, peace instead of strife, success instead of failure, light instead of darkness, and confidence instead of fear. Most successful people and innovators have had deep understanding of how the conscious and subconscious mind works together. This is what gave them the power to accomplish their dreams.

Your subconscious mind is subject to the conscious mind. That is why it is called subconscious or subjective. In this way, your conscious mind is the one in control. So it can tell the subconscious mind what to do. It must obey because it is subject to its command. It responds to the nature of your thoughts, that is, it is reactive when your conscious mind is full of fear, worry, and anxiety. Negative emotions are created in your subconscious mind. These then flood the conscious mind with a sense of panic and despair. When this happens to you, you can use oppositional thinking to affirm confidence, and your subconscious mind releases the negative emotions.

Your subjective mind is aware of its environment, but not by means of physical senses. It perceives by intuition. It is the seat of emotions and storehouse of memories. It performs its highest functions when your objective senses are not functioning. That intelligence makes itself known when the objective mind is suspended or in a sleepy, drowsy state. As you think about it, even when you are asleep, this system controls all the bodily functions. You can feed the message into this system when you want to get up from sleep. Most of the time, it works like magic.

A vast majority of your mental life is subconscious. If you fail to make use of this great power, you condemn yourself to live within very narrow limits. Your subconscious mind is at work all day long. It maintains all vital functions of the body. It is always trying to help and preserve you from harm. It is in touch with infinite life and boundless wisdom, and its impulses and ideas are always life-preserving. The great aspirations, inspirations, and visions for a nobler life spring from the subconscious, but you can condition and cultivate them through the conscious thoughts you feed your subconscious with. Your most profound convictions are those you cannot argue about rationally because they come from your subconscious, not your conscious mind.

Your subconscious speaks to you in intuitions, impulses, urges, and ideas. It is always telling you to transcend, grow, and move forward to greater heights. The urge to love or save the lives of others comes from the depths of your subconscious.

Get Results You Desire

To get a complete picture of how the mind works, it's important to know how it controls bodily functions. The interaction of your conscious and subconscious mind requires a similar interaction between the corresponding systems of nerves. The cerebrospinal or voluntary system is the organ of the conscious mind. The autonomic system is the organ of the subconscious mind. The voluntary nervous system is the channel through which you receive conscious perception by means of your physical senses and exercise voluntary control over the movement of your body. This system has its control center in the cerebral cortex of the brain.

The autonomic nervous system has its centers of activity in the other parts of the brain, including the cerebellum, and brainstem.[15] These organs have their own connections to the major systems of the body and support their vital functions even when conscious awareness is absent.

The two systems may work separately or in tandem. When a perception of danger arrives at the switching center in the cerebellum, messages are sent both to the conscious and subconscious. The person's defensive abilities may start to respond to the danger even before the danger is consciously noted and evaluated.

Nimble Jack confided to Dr. Molly that the creation of new product line in his organization was the result of his ability to tap the inexhaustible reservoir of his subconscious mind with the task of developing a gimmick for it. Through brainstorming every day shortly before going to sleep and just after getting out of bed, the whole puzzle on how to market his idea came to him piece by piece.

You can use this great power of your subconscious mind to develop any leadership quality or get any results that you desire. You can do this at any time of the day, but the best time is in the evening when you are going to sleep or shortly after waking up in the morning. Each night, as you go to sleep, enter into a drowsy, meditative state, the condition likened to sleep. Focus your attention on the results or quality desired. What you need to do in order to avoid failure is to accept your idea or request. It responds to your faith or conscious mind acceptance. Feel the reality of your request and be confident about it. The law of your mind will execute your plan. If you turn over your request with faith and confidence, your subconscious will take over and answer for you.

Lack of confidence and too much effort could lead to failure. So you have to avoid conflict between the conscious and subconscious. Whenever the subconscious

---

15   Charles Haanel, *The Master Key System.*

mind accepts an idea, it immediately begins to execute it. It uses its infinite resources to that end. It mobilizes all the mental and spiritual laws of your deeper mind. This law is true for both good and bad ideas. Consequently, if you use your subconscious negatively, it brings failure and confusion. When you use it constructively, it brings success and peace of mind.

Decree whatever you want and stay relaxed. The all-wise subconscious mind will deliver it to you. Whatever you wish to succeed in (good health, prosperity, or peace of mind), use your imagination, not willpower. Visualize the end because you have to see what the end result will be. Get the feel of the happy ending. The law of attraction has it that this will put you in the creative frequency.

Simply put, in order to stay healthy, picture yourself without the ailment. Then imagine the emotional gratification of the freedom state without the ailment. Genuinely believe that it is already happening. Don't worry about how it will happen.

Focus your attention on the means to obtain your desire, not on the obstacle. Strive for a harmonious agreement between your conscious and subconscious on the mental image of your desire. When there is no longer any disagreement between the two parts of your mind, your wish will be answered. You can minimize conflict between your wish and imagination by entering into a drowsy state that brings all effort to a minimum. When in a sleepy state, the conscious mind is submerged to a great extent. The best time to impregnate your subconscious with a task is just prior to sleep. The highest degree of outcropping of the subconscious occurs just before going to sleep and just after we awaken. In this state, the negative thoughts and imagery that tend to neutralize your desire and prevent your acceptance by your subconscious mind no longer present themselves. When you imagine the reality of the fulfilled desire and feel the thrill of accomplishment, your subconscious brings about the realization of your desire.

Behaviorism

Many people say that behavior is half attitude. I strongly believe that part of being a realist is to recognize the fact that there are so many things that we cannot change. The one thing you can change becomes your attitude. You can then use your positive mental attitude to handle the things you cannot do anything about.

This is the theory that human behavior is determined by conditioning rather than by thoughts or feelings and psychological disorders are best treated by altering behavior patterns. You have probably heard the phrase that psychology is half-habit and half-attitude. You must get in touch with your basic impulses because it has the answer to every difficult situation, be it a new discovery you want to make, a bad habit you want to break, a new habit you want to instill, or something you are afraid of.

Habit is a function of your subconscious mind. You learned to drive a car by consciously doing the appropriate actions repeatedly until they established tracks in your subconscious mind. Then the automatic habit of the subconscious took over. Driving becomes a habit because we do not think about it anymore. If you do, it's very minimal thinking. Most of it is automatic.

If you create your own habit, it follows that you are free to choose good or bad habits. If you repeat a negative thought or action over a period of time, you will place yourself under the compulsion of a habit. The law of your subconscious is compulsion. You need about three weeks to instill a new habit.

Skill Learning and Intelligence

Not all types of learning have to do with absorbing new information. Many types of learning involve doing something and achieving mastery of the thing so it becomes automatic and we no longer have to think about doing it. A fluent reader does not have to look at each word in sentence. Instead, he or she looks directly at two words in the middle of the sentence and recognizes the others instantly by their shape. Someone who is not very good at reading has to decipher every single word. Thus, the expert does the action automatically without thinking. Because the person does not have to think about specific actions, this leaves him or her free to concentrate on other aspects of what he or she is doing, such as thinking about the meaning of the story he or she is reading.

Look at the parts of the brain (Figure 3.1). An action that has been automated is actually controlled by a different part of the brain than an action we have to think about.

Linguistic Intelligence	Understanding of language and how we use it
Musical Intelligence	Musical appreciation as well as aptitude for performing and composing music
Mathematical-Logical Intelligence	Understanding of calculation and logical reasoning
Spatial Intelligence	Aptitude for art and design as well as finding your way around
Bodily Kinesthetic Intelligence	Understanding physical skills, like sport, dancing, and other aspects of movement
Interpersonal Intelligence	Aptitude for interacting with people socially and sensitively9
Intrapersonal Intelligence	Understanding your own personal self and abilities

Table 3.1 Gardner's Seven Intelligences

The cerebrum is the part of the brain that we think with and receives information from our senses, including the body. It has an area that is used for deliberate movement when we consciously decide to move a particular part of the body. This area is known as the motor area, and it is on top of the brain, next to the sensory area that receives bodily feelings.

The area of the brain that coordinates skilled movements is known as the cerebellum. It is concerned with spontaneous movements. If you decide to pick up an object, you do not think about it. The cerebellum coordinates all the movements needed to make that happen.

When a set of actions becomes automated, the control moves from the cerebrum to the cerebellum. Someone who is learning an action, such as driving, will become easily flustered because he or she is thinking about every little action required to complete the task. As we are more practiced, however, those actions become second nature. This, in turn, leaves the cerebrum free to concentrate on other tasks. Skills become automated through practice. With enough practice, people become fluent in many mental skills. And it is generalized mental skills that we are talking of when we talk about the human quality of intelligence.

Leadership is a composite skill for better life mastery. Like all skills, it's learned by use of your mind. Because we influence people through their thoughts and actions, in order to be effective at it, we have to know how to tap into our own mental power as well.

Intelligence consists of grasping the essence of a situation and responding appropriately to them. The word *intelligence* could be used to mean different things. We are sometimes talking about someone who is very quick to grasp facts and make good decisions, but we are sometimes talking about someone who is a deep thinker and can see into problems more deeply than the rest of us. Gardner proposed that there isn't a single thing called intelligence. What we are actually referring to is a set of seven entirely different intelligences. The seven types are listed in Table 3.1.

Each of these types, according to Gardner, is completely separate. Most people that we would call "intelligent" have a combination of these different abilities, but some are particularly good at only one or two and not at the others. A musical genius may have one type of intelligence, but is quite ordinary in other aspects. An idiot savant is someone who is well below average intelligence in most respects, but has one outstanding ability, for example, to calculate or to remember.

Gardner drew much of his evidence from biographies of high-achieving people, but notice that social influences are important in developing and exercising certain kinds of intelligence. What's more, most people who achieve outstanding ability in any area have surely had at least one person who encouraged them. Leading is both science and art. The best evidence is that most people who achieve outstanding ability in any area have usually had at least one person who encouraged them.

Chris Widener "observes that character and skill are the two main reasons why a follower may decide to follow a particular leader."[16] He further explains that you should position yourself in such a manner that the follower perceives you as worthy of being followed. Surveys show that followers prefer to follow someone who shows their values, principles, philosophies, and priorities. People also like to follow someone who is deemed a stronger leader than themselves.

Problem Solving

The greatest skill of all is to learn how to stay focused. This greatly enhances your chance for completing tasks. The best way to approach any problem is to use familiar techniques and skills, not by guessing. When you do not have tried and proven methods to apply in problem-solving, you can use some of the techniques described in this book, including visualization, to change your all-wise subconscious mind to figure out the answer for you. Nothing happens by chance in either the spiritual or physical world. There are laws and principles linked together by the universal intelligence that had neither time nor space.

This is a great problem-solver. You can use this technique in any walk of life, medicine, research, business, and personal. Simply ask, "What are the options?" Then let your mind wander. It stimulates the brain and unlocks its creativity and genius, especially with a pressing problem. When faced with great pressure or pushed out of your comfort zone, adrenaline shuts off. You go into the deep and all-wise subconscious and end up with very interesting

16   Chris Widener

solutions for your problem. This technique clarifies your vision. Once you lay out the different options, then you can see the big picture.

Charles Haanel, in his master key system, suggests that this technique works best when you do it in writing.[17] It stimulates the brain to be more creative. So get a piece of paper. Write down as many options as possible to solving the problem.

I use this method in my practice to great effect. I know the door for change in people's lives swings outwards. Also, if only they could think-act-feel to make a difference, people have the bigger picture of what is happening to their lives. They are the only ones who can change their mental state. I only listen to see whether I could redirect them to something they may be overlooking and/or sympathize or empathize, but the solution is ultimately in their hands. So, quite often, in complex issues, I hand the pen and paper to them and give them time to brainstorm and instruct them on how to use the technique. Most often, I am quite positively surprised at the solutions that people can bring up for a seemingly complicated problem.

The Magnet

To be a magnet is to draw what you desire onto yourself, not by chasing it. This is consistent with how the mind works, so, in order to possess the quality of confidence, you start by thinking, acting, and feeling confident. Similarly, if you want to be loved, you have to be lovable. You do this by thinking, acting, and feeling as though you love. So simply create a blueprint for any leadership quality that you wish to develop and practice to great effect until it becomes second nature. You could, just as Nimble Jack did, use as many of these qualities that you desire to create affirmations by using some of the techniques I have discussed to imbue your subconscious.

Reactivity reinforces psychological resistance, which limits your ability to get into harmony with the universal intelligence, the greatest creative force. So you begin to see the big picture, and your focus changes from "me" to "we." As you

---

17   Charles Haanel: The Master Key System

detach yourself from outcomes, your voice takes a softer tone. You become less defensive, less critical of others, and more risk-taking.

As we have seen, constantly challenge your subconscious mind with your blueprint or desired outcome. Just calmly think over what you want and visualize it coming to fruition from this moment forward. Again, use no effort. Your conscious mind is like a camera. Do not try to push too hard. Just present the idea as a brief affirmation, a simple phrase. The subconscious mind is like the film that develops or releases the idea that becomes a reality or full picture.

There is always a direct response from the infinite intelligence of your subconscious mind to your conscious thinking. The fundamental and most far-reaching activity in life is that which you build into your mentality every waking hour. Your thought is silent and invisible, but it is real. So your thoughts represent your life story, identity, heroic mission, personality, or whatever you wish to create.

Moment by moment, you can build radiant success by the thoughts you think, the beliefs you accept, and the scenes you rehearse in your mind. Act as though you are, and you will be. The Bible puts it very clearly. It shall be opened to you when you knock, and you shall find that for which you are searching. This underscores the teachings of mental and spiritual laws.

Buddha observed that what we are is a result of our thoughts. Our thoughts are the causes, and our external world is the effects. You must ask believing if you are to receive. Your mind moves from the thought to the thing. You must reach the point of acceptance in your mind, an undisputed state of agreement. The feeling of joy and assurance of the accomplishment of your desire should accompany this contemplation.

It's up to you whether you need a new leadership quality or heroic mission. These basic rules will undoubtedly help you play your best game in life. Many people out there know nothing about the law of gravity, but the gravitational pull acts on them just the same. Whether you know it or not, your lack of knowledge of the social graces or how your world works stifles your chances of moving ahead. Awareness always precedes action. By redirecting your conscious mind to dwell upon virtues rather than vices, your subconscious mind will accept your blueprint and bring all of these things to pass.

A lot of research shows that integrity is arguably the number-one leadership quality. People want someone who is reliable. Being trustworthy means that your followers can trust your word regarding who you say you are or what you stand for. If you are not believable, then everything else you claim is open to question. So you're neither reliable nor authentic. This is why being faithful and true to yourself and your values is fundamental to being a great leader.

So why is one person a success and another is a failure? Most of the answer is in the fact that one of them learned how to use his or her most precious possession, the mind. The other did not. What you truly believe in and feel strongly about, now you know how to fill up yourself with it until you being to overflow. That is how you become a magnet of your desires. You are a magnet full of energy, ideas, ambition, and confidence. You come to the realization that life belongs to the bold and meek. You start to think like a winner. Losers, on the contrary, do not believe in themselves, so they exercise false humility. They are so timid that any bold move is perceived as arrogance. Consequently, they are energetically flat and melancholic perfectionists and full of fears, cynicism, and doubt.

I cannot stress enough how important using your mind is. It's the great master that many people don't know how to exploit. The foundation for everything in your life, spiritual or physical, is laid in this storehouse. It's a small wonder that, when it's gone, you're finished, too. Your world is simply your mirror, but where is the mirror? It's in the words you use and your actions. The character and personality that are ascribed to you emanate from this storehouse.

As a physician, I know immediately when I am dealing with an autistic child, just from the way he or she relates, his or her mannerisms, or how he or she behaves. You can quickly surmise one's behavior and character, but you need to have knowledge of the different types of personalities.

A positive mental attitude goes hand in hand with optimism and hope. It is imagining and expecting the best, but, at the same time, accepting and preparing for the worst-case scenario. It frees up wasted energy on worrying or brooding about the past or things that do not come to fruition. Positive thoughts are buoyant and very uplifting, as opposed to negative thoughts that sap your energy.

A positive mental attitude can transcend anything. No matter how badly you have been treated, if you genuinely decide to let go and move forward, you will. It is a great psychological release. It frees up the wasted energy that holds you back and then puts you in harmony with the universal intelligence. Surveys have shown that people with positive mental attitudes are better problem-solvers. They are more content and live longer and healthier lives.

Victor Frankl's book on man's search for meaning talks about personal suffering and eyewitness accounts of the excruciating pain inflicted on fellow inmates while he was imprisoned at Auschwitz for five years. Frankl observed that those who could emotionally survive their surroundings were those who could imagine themselves free to transcend the suffering and find a meaningful life despite the circumstances.

In 1942, Frankl, a recently married doctor, was arrested, separated from the rest of his family, and sent to the concentration camp. While in the prison camp, he secretly worked on a manuscript and imagined reuniting with his family. Instead of focusing on his lost purpose, Frankl created one. To survive the horrors, people have to look into the future. This future would have been doomed if he had lost faith.

Faith is the greatest hope builder. Expecting the best and establishing competence and mastery creates significance and meaning to fill the existential vacuum. Another important reason why hope is crucial is because we never have answers for all the problems so learning how to handle problems is important.

Difficult life events or crises bring the best or worst out of people. It's no wonder that most great leaders have faced great adversities in their lives. Crises push people out of their comfort zone, which puts enormous pressure on them. The urgency makes them more creative and physiologically more tuned into the basic impulses. Their instincts or intuition get stimulated, and it can multiply their ability. Hormones, like adrenaline, are very powerful, and they act instantaneously with little or no thought. When you are pushed out of your comfort zone, it's easier to make an emotional connection too, and it's quite often for the simple reason that there is no choice. Look at Frankl's situation. He did not have the power to reverse the situation in a physical way, so he used his attitude to conquer adversity. He deliberately chose not to dwell on the apparent failure.

Another popular psychiatrist, Karl Menninger, also observed that attitude is more powerful than facts. An attitude of optimism is very uplifting all the time but especially in times of difficulty. When you are optimistic, you still recognize the failure or potential failure, but you choose to dwell on something positive. No matter how dire the circumstances are, there can always be something positive to fixate your mind on. It moves you forward into the future rather than wallow in self-pity. Many problems do not have answers. Shifting your mind-set becomes very important.

IV. Combating Negative Behavior

The focus of leadership is modeling, as well as helping people fulfill their potential.

Gloria Blacklock

Chapter Four

Combating Negative Behavior

Self-confidence

I cannot overstate how important this is to your life. Staying focused is your first rule of success. Marsha went to see Dr. Molly because she was lying awake for a week without sleeping. She explained her previous boyfriend had asked for the birth certificate of their daughter, so she concluded that he wanted to take her to the United States. They had separated many years ago, and a custody battle was looming. She had to take stress leave for six months because she could not cope both at home and at work. She could not focus, so she did not get tasks completed at work. She was at the brink of a nervous breakdown. Marsha was totally free of any medical pathology, yet she could not focus or sleep. She had no pep.

These are real problems. A person is diagnosed with cancer. You lose your loved one. You are laid off from work. The key to handling these problems without clear solutions is found in developing coping mechanisms and using some of the techniques described to control your mind. The optimistic and selfless attitudes are very helpful because, in that way, you do not take things personally. You can turn yourself into a shouting optimist.

Jim Rohn, author and motivational speaker, defines leadership as "the challenge to be something better than mediocre, a step above, not from an ego standpoint but to lift up someone else. In order to do that, you have to be on higher ground."[18]

---

18   Jim Rohn, , *The Secret to Millionaire Success.*

The heroic mission is a composite of vision and imagery of the extraordinary. It's having a clear picture of where you want to go, the end game. It's taking a challenge of where you want to go. As a physician, I interview scores of people every day. Intuitively, I have come to understand why some people are successful and others are not. Confidence is a good example here because it is a very important leadership quality. Hardly a quality determines how you conduct your life more than self-confidence. This is probably why your sense of security is your best source of psychological strength and stability. A lot of fear comes from lack of confidence or insecurity. This puts a ceiling on how far you progress in life, your passion, and energy. When you feel confident, you are more likely to be an active agent in your life, making your own choices as opposed to being passive. In that way, you are deliberately influencing what may happen in each situation.

Lack of confidence, therefore, is likely to refuel anxiety and procrastination because you are more likely to anticipate pain or failure rather than success in a given situation. Because like attracts like, as in the Law of Attraction, you will draw more psychological pain and failure to yourself. There's no higher leverage than psychologically believing that you can. Thinking that the sky is the only limit you have opens endless possibilities. This is the winning attitude. Cultivate the habit to always stay as cool as a cucumber.

Developing this mental toughness is the key to handling difficult situations. The greatest factor in determining how you handle yourself is your attitude. Be open-minded. Always respond with, "Yes, I can do it!" Your default state of mind should be cool and lacking in drama.

You do not have control over all that happens to you, but you can anticipate outcomes and how to deal with them. You should try to maintain a positive attitude and look for opportunities in any outcome because you do not have control over everything.

You can see why selflessness is a great attitude to possess. It comes from being egoless. Selfless people tend to be very gracious or blame-free. Thus, there is a no-blame policy in the team they lead. This is a great value of a leader. When you operate from here, you are cool and levelheaded. Only then can you focus on your goal. With this kind of attitude, even fire burning behind you doesn't matter. All the hysteria and commotion in the background avails to nothing.

You have the power to respond to any situation with love and compassion or fear and control. You can see the great paradigm shift between the two poles: compassion or fear. In our imagination, we expect the worst will happen. So how you respond changes your frame of mind. A positive, compassionate response puts you in a positive frame of mind while a fearful one puts you in a negative frame of mind.

Your body knows the difference when you respond from a position of compassion and confidence. The body senses that you are in for a fight, so it uses the same adrenaline to prepare you for action. Your vitality is restored rather than letting it evaporate. As a leader, to be able to be a light source and shine for others to follow, you have to be on higher ground. Nothing makes you lose your ground like psychological resistance. It's like taking air out of the balloon.

Fear and Anxiety

Mrs. Johnston was seeing Dr. Molly because she was having trouble sleeping. Her headaches became worse. She could not get out of the house. She decided she was never going to fly anymore. Her husband accompanied her because he very much wanted to solve these problems so they could vacation together abroad.

Dr. Molly felt badly for Mr. Johnston as the man tried to argue logically. He was very frustrated and rightly so. He had taken to travelling alone for many years. The time had come, and he was going to do something about it. Mrs. Johnston had lost a son to a flight accident, and she did not want the same thing to happen to her. Dr. Molly did not argue with her because most of her problem was with her subconscious mind, not in her conscious or super-conscious mind. He would have to try to desensitize her. It would take a long time, and it might still not work.

Worry and anxiety come from fear. Fear is often based on something that may happen, a perceived danger. Thus, it is poor use of imagination because you expect the worst will happen rather than the best. Fear is an emotion, the body's reaction to your mind. So examples could be multiplied here, for example, fear of being hurt in a plane crash as in Mrs. Johnston's case. But fear of abandonment, phobia, failure, and rejection are very common as well.

Part of the solution is to become egoless. When you are fixated on the self-centered elements of your mind, the ego runs your life. It is very vulnerable and sees itself as constantly under threat. So it thinks it needs self-preservation. But, if you focus too much on the manifestations of your ego, you feel the need to be right all the time.

You can see in Mrs. Johnston's situation that the exaggerated risk of a plane crash is well formed and integrated as part of her identity. She needs a very strong paradigm shift here. The problem here is that her level of risk from dying from a plane crash is exaggerated way out of proportion. Comparatively, more people die from car accidents than plane crashes. However, this reality does not change her false belief of an overly exaggerated danger of flying. This fear of death from flying is at the core of her anxiety even though it's not real.

The fear emotion can be a response to an actual event. This is accompanied by the interpretation as either good or bad. If you have bonds with the object of a situation, then you are affected. Think how you would respond to the news of a stolen car when it's yours or someone else's. Think how you respond to the news of an earthquake in a foreign country. If you had somebody from your own family visiting there, your response would be different.

Eckhart Tolle suggests that you dissolve these ego manifestations by bringing them into the light of awareness.[19] The subconscious mind does not distinguish between fiction and reality. The conscious mind filters information as right or wrong, fearful or not.

An instinctive response is the body's direct response to an external situation. An emotion, on the other hand, is the body's response to a thought. Thus,

---

19   Eckhart Tolle, *A New Earth.*

fear is a psycho-emotional condition that is not based on reality. Because the subconscious mind does not distinguish between fantasy and reality, you get exactly the same effect whether your thought is based on reality or not. This is why belief is so strong.

In order to become egoless, do not identify with ego manifestations. In this way, being right or wrong makes no difference to your sense of self as you become selfless. This dissolves the psychological resistance that holds you back. Again, these include negative emotions, fear, envy, jealousy, judgment, criticism, defensiveness, and so on.

You gain a measure of true power as you discover that it comes from within, not from outside. You cease from controlling behavior that only escalates ego manifestations. You then become like the light that radiates gentleness, gratitude, grace, and compassion. This is peace of mind. When you truly feel secure, you can enjoy your life as you can focus on designing it so that your actions match your intentions. Rather than live by default, embrace anything.

Balance is good both professionally and personally. You cannot be happy if you are stressed out. Exercise, good sleep, and laughter are the best relievers of stress. Stress leads to burnout, insomnia, and loss of vitality. There is no better rock in your life than family or friends. But make yourself somebody that people can lean on as well.

By far, the greatest hope-builder is faith and God. It's your greatest rock. You can double your bottom line by cutting down the amount of time spent per service. This may not reduce the quality of your service because spending more time does not necessarily equal better quality.

Emotional Pain

Mr. Bensan, a sixty-year-old retired man, had lost his wife two years ago He was suffering from insomnia. He felt lonely, and he had a brooding fixation on dying all the time. He had no pep. The first question he asked when he went to Dr. Molly for guidance was, "How do I get out of this mess?" Dr. Molly suggested the brainstorming technique as it gives lot of insight on what the real issues are. It also helps define what the problem is before launching into the solution.

In the end, it was very clear to both of them that he was living in isolation. He was just existing. He confided that he had made lots of money and felt it was time to enjoy being retired, but he found himself out of touch with most of his friends who were still working. His children were grown and gone as well. The hole in his life was so big that, many times during the day, he saw nothing but gloom. He didn't see any way out other than just putting an end to the whole mess.

The emotional pain here was very obvious. The real question was, "How did he get out of the pit?" His insight was still intact, so he asked the right question right at the beginning. He knew that things were not going well. He had to undergo a major paradigm shift. This is the go-home-and-die mentality. Without a worthy heroic mission and goals to stand for, it stifles ambition and creativity. There was no passion to carry him through, so his mind went to sleep. Rather than think of his values and align them with his goals to have a heroic mission, something he could stand for, he spent time brooding over all of the negative things of the world rather than focus on the great things he wanted to achieve. He had no purpose behind the purpose, as Denis Waitley calls it. This is something that positively impacts the society.

Mr. Bensan did not know what significance meant. He made enough money, so he retired. Money buys a lot of freedom, but the noble purpose always trumps money. Mr. Bensan was encouraged to reinvent himself. He had to do many things to pull himself out of the funk. He had to renegotiate his life by changing his mentality regarding a whole lot of things.

One of his fears was losing his property, including his house, to a new partner. He wanted his children to benefit from it. He decided he would sign a prenuptial agreement before starting a new relationship. In that way, they could both walk away without losing what they owned. He confided to Dr. Molly that one of his sons was creamed when he separated from his wife. He said that, with a 50 percent divorce rate in North America, it was a smart thing to do. Dr. Molly told

Mr. Bensan that, if a prenuptial agreement alleviated his paranoia, then it was up to him.

Mr. Bensan started dating. He freed up a lot of his energy that a fear of the unknown had locked in. Part of the rub in all of this was that Mr. Bensan did not fully grieve his wife when she died. So he was encouraged to take a step in that direction. He attended bereavement sessions and learned a lot about grieving. After the shock of the event, he was stuck in the denial stage. He never explored the whole situation. He simply repressed the negative emotions rather than acknowledge it and let it go. Many months of counseling and encouraging him to talk to anybody who was ready to listen to him freed up all of the energy that was locked in the negative emotions. He came to accept the loss as it was and decided to move forward.

Even a plan that could be described as pitiful is often better than none. Mr. Bensan was a consummate example of an aimless man. He basically just existed. Until he had to sit down for months of counseling, redefine what his values were, and align some major goals with them, he could not do anything. That fear was the main factor that kept him back.

Paranoia

Sam said, "I believe that my number is coming up." He believed a truck driver would fall asleep behind the wheel and hit him head-on. The justification was scanty to say the least. His wife was at the interview and observed that, whenever she was on the phone with someone, he always thought they were saying something nasty about him. His social fabric, family, and work were falling apart. The substance as well as the tone of his delivery was pitiful. His psychological and emotional pain was palpable.

There was a need for Sam to understand what the problem was and develop a long-term change in behavior. He stopped working because he was afraid a truck was going to hit him. How do you address this kind of problem? The possibility of the danger is described here, but what are the odds that this will happen? The urgent need for both a psychiatrist and psychologist was obvious, but the key to my message here is that learning how to control his mind could sidestep the intensity of this paranoia. Hence, he could really avoid some of the emotional pain that comes out of this kind of negative thinking, a major factor that holds people back.

Nobody's life is entirely free of sorrow. Thus, learning how to live with it is important. Some human pain is unnecessary. It is self-created as long as the unobserved mind runs your life. The psychological and emotional pain is often some form of nonacceptance, some form of unconscious resistance to what is. On the level of thought, the resistance is some form of judgment. On the emotional level, it's some form of negativity. The intensity of the pain depends on the degree of resistance. This, in turn, depends on how strongly you are indentified with your mind. The more you are identified with your mind, the more you suffer emotionally.

So stay alert and present at that time. Watch whatever you feel within rather than be taken over by it. This is a very easy way to transcend pain or pleasure. Remember that we do everything for one of two reasons: to avoid pain or to gain pleasure. You stay in touch with our impulse or instinct.

Logic and facts are important, but let your subconscious toss issues around. In that way, you get in touch with your basic impulses. These mechanisms instantly know what you are feeling or thinking, and they pick up the vibes with the beat of the heart.

So staying alert helps you to no longer identify with your ego manifestations, which ultimately bring pain. You have believed that this self-made fantasy of your ego is who you are. Take a leap by a paradigm shift, leaving this unhappy self behind you. Some people like familiarity, even if it gives them pain. They prefer it over the new and unfamiliar or unknown. When you choose to stay alert, you can observe the attachment to your pain. This psychological resistance will cease if you make it conscious. This sustained attention is the light of your presence that dissolves the darkness of negative emotion.

So you can zap the negative thought. But remember that, in very deep, unconscious fear of paranoid proportions or loss of a loved one, you need structured behavior change and desensitization and bereavement counseling as part of the intervention.

Effects of Stress

Stress affects your body as a whole. It's all chemistry, so your blood pressure and pulse shut down. This puts a strain on the heart, which could then lead to chest pains. Strain is also put on all the organs of your body, including increases in your cortisone level, which lowers your immunity and increases your chance for developing diabetes. Extremely high blood pressure levels can also increase your risk for strokes. Stress can also cause severe weight gain and prevent you from sleeping.

Stress definitely kills. Again, stress-causing fear is poor imagination, where you expect the worst. So learn to expect the best to eliminate this aspect of worry that leads to stress and anxiety. Your conscious mind filters information that gets stored in the subconscious mind as good or bad. A mind pattern is created that responds spontaneously without necessarily thinking or with very minimal thinking.

This part of the brain is limited to the autonomic nervous system that picks up impulses from within and acts spontaneously. The problem with fear is that it's an emotional reaction that is not based on reality. The dilemma is that the subconscious mind cannot distinguish between fiction and reality. If you believe an elephant is sitting under your bed, it has the same effects on you whether it's there or not. Sam believed a truck driver was going to hit him head-on and kill him. While this sounds like a stretch to a rational mind, Sam exaggerated this possibility, and this was the cause of his neurosis.

Saving Your Energy

One of Dr. Molly's clients used oppositional thinking to great effect. Oppositional thinking is simply substituting a positive thought for a negative one. Paul had a motor vehicle accident and lost two front teeth. He put a positive affirmation in his mind. He thought and felt that he was a hockey player. He then associated a million dollars with being a hockey player. This sounds like a stretch, but it psyches him up.

Energy goes where there is attention. The Law of Attraction simply states that you get what you focus on. In other words, you manifest what you think about. So focus on what you want to experience. Thought is energy in motion.[20] Humans are simply energy. So knowing how to recycle energy from spiritual, emotional, and psychological thinking is crucial.

You are either operating at a negative, neutral, or positive energy. You can determine where you want to be. Simply focus on what you want. If you want good health, focus on healing. Think, act, and feel about good health. That's how you heal yourself from any ailment. Think about having a healthy heart rather than worry about having a heart attack. This is because what you resist persists. You manifest what you feel and think.

Repression occurs when you resist negative emotions, too. Welcome or acknowledge your emotions and then let go. If you feel like crying, do so because it releases a lot of tension. If something happens to you that you do not like, do not deny it. If you lose a loved one, accept that it happened, psychologically and factually. We think that losing a loved one is not good. Most people try to resist it. As you do, the emotion persists rather than go away. When you acknowledge the loss and anger, it's an effective way of releasing it.

In order to move forward, you may need to use other techniques like oppositional thinking. It's simply replacing a negative thought with a positive one. Once you entertain the fact that your current thought or situation is not what you want to experience, you have to shift attention to what you want to experience. You have to change the old script when you create a new affirmation. Then intone

---

20   Eckhart Tolle, *A New Earth.*

your subconscious mind with it through constant practice on a daily basis. The subconscious is your seat of long-term memory. Here is a simple affirmation for a loss. "I see any job loss as a blessing in disguise because I can now focus on looking for my dream job."

Hardly anything takes away your vitality like negative emotions. Whatever happens, fall back to your basic theme of the can-do attitude. Keep your spirits up, charge forward, and achieve your dreams. Be simply unstoppable.

V. Growing Up & Self-Leadership

Everything rises and falls on leadership.

John C. Maxwell

Chapter Five

Growing Up and Self-leadership

Welcome Adversity

Going through adversity taught me a lot on how to deal with life's challenges. My father was not willing to educate me through school. Consequently, I had no choice but to think of alternative options on how to support myself financially through school. From an early age, I had to learn how to be self-reliant and take initiative in getting things done.

I was born in a village called Awing, Cameroon, in West Africa. My father, Joseph, is a businessman. Susan, my mother, is a perfect homemaker. I left the village and went to the city to attend primary school with George, my eldest brother, who lived in Bamenda and was working with the military. He is the first in line. I am the fourth in a nuclear family of nine. It was customary that, during holidays, we all come home and help our father in his multiple businesses to keep his empire going. He has coffee plantations, herds of cattle, and real estate, to name a few.

When I was in my teens, I spent my three-month holiday, along with other stepbrothers, helping my father, but not with the intention of making money. However, we made him lots of money. I did everything from climbing up the mountains and feeding salt to the cattle, working in the coffee plantations, harvesting corn, and helping him lend as much money as possible in his money-lending business.

The lending business is sort of like trade by barter. If somebody needs money, he or she can see my father, and my father would give him or her money.

During harvesting season, the farmer would then bring him produce, coffee, or cattle that he would sell, depending on his trade.

The profit margins went more than wonderfully. So my father made lots of money off the backs of the poor. I have hardly seen anybody much wiser than my father is in negotiating deals. He had leverage for being rich, but he was naturally very intelligent and wise in business. And making money is his only passion.

My greatest revelation would come at the end of this three-month holiday. My father had many children now. He had stacks of money in front of him. He gave hundreds of dollars each to the other children. When my turn came, he gave me five Canadian dollars. This was just enough to pay for my transport back to school. You could not dare argue with him. You had only one option, conform and ask no questions. I went into my mother's house and showed her. Tears were rolling down my cheeks. Being a master diplomat and fearing my father pouncing on her, she did not say a word.

At the time, I did not know that this was a major turning point in my life. This was a rallying cry for me because not everybody in the family agreed with my father. They thought he went too far.

Having a big family with scores of people, it's hard to be impartial. But seeing five dollars given to one kid and hundreds to the others, the difference is like day and night. He gave me a good reason to break from the crowd, and I became the self-reliant person that I am to this day. It was a wake-up call for me to become independent. The story broke in the family and went across the whole village. It was not good for him, being the village tycoon.

The five dollars could only pay my transport back to the city. Then I had to struggle by myself, borrowing and trying all sorts of business ventures, even during school, to pay for my education. Martin is the one brother who tried to help me in school. He was a very good coach in guiding me how to structure my time between business and school. When I returned to the city, I was still in shock. For three days, I lay in bed awake, just thinking. I ate very little food during those three days.

I weighed all the options. I decided not to go to the village during the holidays. I would spend my time doing holiday jobs and creating my own businesses in order to make money and pay for my own education.

I was one of the first to break away from my father's iron clasp dictatorship that gave him so much undue influence over everybody else. Even as a man working in the city, he was the priority of what you earned, not your family. You had to satisfy him first. Otherwise, you were in the black book. If any of his sons did not send him money every month, he was in trouble. When I stopped going to the village and helping him, nobody blamed me because they were aware of how he treated me very unfairly.

Knowing I was on my own, this only helped inspire me to work harder, reflect deeper, and become more streetwise and bold as well. The businesses I tried to create during my spare time made me very time-conscious.

Little did I know, those seemingly little things I did would contribute significantly both to who and what I am today. I learned so many lessons from going out to the bigger world and struggling for myself. This is how I gained my passion for business and helping people. I spontaneously became more streetwise, bold, imaginative, and a good steward for time. You need these major qualities to succeed in the real world.

I noticed that most of my stepbrothers who were handed everything they needed never garnered any of these qualities. They became so ingrown that all they wanted was to be like our father. They could not use the two most important gifts of all: intelligence and time. Each time they were faced with a problem, they ran back home to get money from my father. I discovered early that smarts and boldness surpass college education in terms of being successful.

Asking somebody to meet you halfway before you help him or her or severing the umbilical cord teaches him or her how to stand on his or her own feet. It teaches someone to think independently and reflect deeply. Then he or she taps into the inner knowing of wisdom that lies dormant and infinite. This is what happened to me when I lay in bed sleepless for three days.

You have to have the ability to grow. You have to have the ability to connect with the infinite intelligence of the universe that lodges in you. To be in harmony with the universe is the mechanism for bringing this great power out of you, as Charles Haanel explains in *The Master Key System*.

When you hand things to people, it kills their initiative and creativity. It breeds laziness, a sense of entitlement, selfishness, boredom, and inaction. The best way people, including children, learn is through experience, inspiration, and osmosis. More importantly in any situation, that will take them out of their comfort zone. You don't learn anything when you are in your comfort zone. We know that necessity is the mother of invention. I know parents who are so protective of their kids that they cannot allow them to go to holiday camp with their peers.

In spite of the affluence with which we live, some very smart parents create situations where the children could have a growing experience. They create a situation where they could come out of their comfort zone from time to time. The examples are endless. Either as individuals or as a group, you can climb a mountain, run a marathon, or take a leadership workshop.

My friend Jim takes his children to work with him. Just doing what he does is a big source of learning through osmosis. His son watches him cut deals with people. Jim also gave two thousand dollars to his son to play on the stock market. These are great opportunities to listen and learn how to observe and think independently. In this way, you participate in life. You have a story to tell. You can really get to know who you are rather than sit on the sidelines and watch life pass you by.

My daughter Ruthie and her friend Nikita are preteens, and they started an online company called Smooth Smoothies. As wise parents, we did not stop them from doing it. That would kill their creativity and ability to think for themselves. I greatly admire those two girls because they have the guts to go from door to door and talk about their business. As a business owner, I know how important marketing skills are in life. By just being able to talk to people about their business, they have overcome the greatest obstacle that keeps many people behind, fear. These two kids did something noble, contributing 25 percent of their proceeds to my foundation, which does poverty relief work.

The most important aspect of your life journey is knowing who you are. It is a never-ending process. When we gain brief moments of harmony with the universal intelligence, we get a glimpse of who we are, which makes our self-image grow. This is why our focus changes in life as we grow. Our picture of the world changes as well. Knowing we are all made in God's image is important. So we are a spiritual being lodged inside a body and possess the same infinite spirit that God possesses, an infinite source of intelligence. Learning how to tap into it is the key. This is why letting anybody tell you that you cannot do something is criminal. It imposes false limits on you. In truth, from a temporal or spatial perspective, there are no limits. You can do anything you can conceive!

Perhaps the greatest lesson I learned from my father was watching him cut deals at a very young age. He always said, "Yes, your balls are big enough." This was the answer to every situation. A customer would come in and describe a seemingly insurmountable problem. With a grin on his face, my father would say yes to the man and let him come and see him. In a few minutes, the man would come out with a smile on his face and high-five my father.

Even as a physician, the most I can do is tune into someone's story, understand what is going on for a particular situation, and then offer potential options to them. In very clear-cut problems, I may say, "If you were my daughter, here is the option I would vote for." It's a very subtle form of influence. You learn not to limit anybody's world. Someone's world is a microcosm of the universe. Only they have the access to it through thinking and feeling. Their words and actions may give us a glimpse into it, but, because people do different things for different reasons, you cannot impose superficial judgments on them. Your best option is to observe and see whatever is as it is. You limit biased interpretations into situations as much as possible. When you start interpreting, you have already bought into a particular school of thought, and that already starts to limit your world or that of your opponent. All you need to do is experience what it is and move forward.

It's such a wonderful release to just accept a situation as it is and move forward. When the crisis happened, I went into shock for three days. It happened right in the beginning of the school year, so I did not have time to go through all the stages of grieving. There was no time for denial, bargaining, or slipping into a depression. I lay in bed awake for three days and realized I was wasting my tears. So I cut to the chase and did what I had to do. I accepted the situation as it was and moved forward.

George, my older brother, felt I should study a trade like carpentry, but I argued I was among the best in school. I wanted to study law in the university, which would pave the way to either practice law or go to the military academy, to fulfill my ultimate goal of being a general. As I look back, being very ambitious and knowing what I wanted motivated me to fight and not give up. If I did not take a strong position about what I wanted my future to be like, maybe I would have bought into George's easy way out.

As it stands, I did very well in school. I was a very popular science student. I won so many presidential awards for being an all-around student. I ended up in medicine because Martin convinced me that it was easier to go into the military academy with a degree in medicine than in law. When I was in medical school, I owned a restaurant and a taxi business. My personal hard work and initiative and a very generous, personal friend, Colonel Mballa, helped me in countless ways to get these businesses started.

When I started these businesses, I did not know that the Cameroonian government would be experiencing such a tough economical crisis and end up completely stopping the payment of all scholarships to medical students. I had the opportunity to give my friends and family members more than just a free lunch. This experience was the turning point in my life. It brought out the giant in me and completely changed my mind-set from dependent to independent.

Adversity is a great hope-builder. Never fight adversity because that leads to internal psychological conflict, which prevents you from fully understanding and accepting who you truly are. When you try to resist rather than welcome and accept it, it knocks you off balance and out of your comfort zone. For some people, a negative experience can be so scary that it numbs their feelings.

When you acknowledge adversity and see it as a stepping-stone, you can emerge stronger from it. It's a great recipe for becoming psychologically secure and full of confidence. Until you understand and accept who you are, you will always be tied to the past. You will lack inner validation, which leaves a void behind. You will always need external validation to fill that void. Your happiness will then depend on it. Other people then hold the key to your happiness. Instead, you should be the one in control.

You have to be well grounded with lots of psychological space. Truly secure people are not people pleasers. Even God doesn't please everybody. You do not have to be a diva, but unconditionally accept who you are. Believe in yourself. It is the true path of success because you can do what you want to do without worrying about what people think about you.

You can respectfully disagree with people and move on without demonizing them. It's even better when you have the maverick moniker. You play by your own rules!

Growing Partnerships

Your world is a mirror of who you are, and it is a microcosm of the universe. A web of partnerships makes your world. When I grew up, I inherited my mother's work ethic. I worked hard, went to university, got educated, and went to medical school. With time, I realized that it's just a good start because it's a means and not an end. As my picture of life grew, I realized there is more to life than just education.

You need your smarts in order to win because you can only manifest what you think, feel, and visualize. You need other people, but it's important to look beyond the surface when networking with others. But all of the planning in the world without the boldness that crowns the action avails to nothing. With most of the people I work with, I always wanted them to feel like an integral part of the dream I stand for. Who they are and what they can do is often more important to me than the degrees they have.

One of the best ways to influence or persuade people is to be convincing, but not try to convince. Show evidence that speaks for itself. Tell your followers the rationale of what you are doing. If they listen, with a resounding yes or no, they will either follow you or leave. The truth is not in the evidence. It's in the way people either look at or connect with something. It's only the individual who can feel and actually think about what truly moves them. Is his or her inner purpose in alignment to what you are proposing? Only that person can tell. You cannot push. When I was about to start my foundation, I interviewed Mr. Torres for my board of directors. He was a very good friend of mine for a very long time, but I did not know him as well as he would come to let me know.

After a long session with him, he just did not understand why a physician should be passionate about poverty relief. In his words, it's the duty of the government. I had a few disappointments like this, but I went forward to speak to other people who believed in my vision. This is much easier than trying to bring the faithless onto your side. Whatever game you are thinking of playing, always know somebody is around the corner and already playing it.

When I first met Lynn, I had no doubt that she would make a good CEO for the Skylimit Corporation. She was very knowledgeable and talented. She knows a lot about the retail industry and money. I have hardly seen anyone more proactive than her.

Barrister Nico Halle is a great friend and mentor. He has been very instrumental in getting this project off the ground. Emmanuel is highly involved, too. He is a human dynamo with lots of ingenuity and innovative thinking. He is a technocrat in the real sense of the word. He is an academic of great repute and a self-made millionaire. Nobody knows how he educated himself through law school and, at the same time, built a business line in cosmetics. Now, with a degree in law, he is going to do post-graduate business administration. His credentials so flatter and encourage me that Nico and I think he deserves a prominent role in this banking institution. He has accepted to be the general manager of Equity Bank Cameroon.

The people mentioned here are some of my heroes and mentors. They teach, encourage, and motivate me, just as much as I try to do for them. I find that true partnership is a two-way street, a symbiosis.

VI. Leadership Milestones

In my model of dynamic influence, you become a human dynamo to best harness your potential.

Dr. Alfred Nkut

Chapter Six

Leadership Milestones

The Model of Dynamic Influence

When it comes to living your purpose, I like the analogy of a dynamo, the device for converting mechanical energy into electrical energy. Living without a purpose is like having a dynamo that is not connected to a lightbulb to deliver electricity, so the energy in the dynamo is wasted, not harnessed. The essence is to align your goals with a wider purpose. Otherwise, you just waste your energy.

My model of dynamic influence likens a leader to a dynamo. A dynamic leader is a human dynamo that generates enthusiasm, new ideas, and much more. He or she is very powerful like a dynamo, too, but, even more importantly, he or she is influential and good at getting things done.

I like this model of dynamic influence because humans are made up of energy. This is very comparable to the dynamo that generates energy, too. In order to be a dynamic leader, you have to harness the energy in such a manner as to create magnetism that is needed to influence either at an individual or team level. We are all connected electromagnetically to the wider perspective called the universe.

You can now see how a dynamic leader channels the power of his followers (just as a dynamo channels the power of the turning wheels) into a more usable and focused power. Putting together the individual energies in order to create unity of vision is crucial in winning either at a personal level or team level.

Many parallels are to be drawn between the leader being a human dynamo. Often, many variables exist in a chemical reaction. When lined up appropriately, a catalyst speeds up the reaction by reducing the activation energy. The potential energy is then transformed to the kinetic energy, the usable form of energy. In the case of the dynamo, mechanical energy is transformed into electrical energy.

The leader often asks the question, "What kind of the variable or leverage do I need in order to positively impact the situation?" Generally speaking, you want to leverage up, but remember your best option may be to sometimes sit quietly with your mouth shut and do nothing! You will sometimes need more than one factor to make things happen. At times, you want to multiply the effect of your effort, like a catalyst does in a chemical reaction. That is, you want to leverage up.

Another important parallel to draw here is that the potential energy in chemical reactions is converted to kinetic energy when the right conditions occur. In like manner, we can release our potential if we possess it. These gifts lie dormant within you and need motivation, inspiration, growth, development, and nurturing in order to make use of them.

So, as a leader, you are supposed to bring out the best from your followers, not only from yourself. Your followers have lots of potential lying dormant within. Part of your role as a leader is to develop and nurture those things in them. This is where modeling and helping people achieve their potential is important.

This model of dynamic influence also emphasizes doing what the situation needs in order to move forward, being adaptable as need be, and always trying to leverage up. Thus, this means looking at things not only as they are, but what they could or should be. You are constantly running through your options and consequences of action or wait-and-see approach for the situation at hand. Rather than pull the trigger with the wrong timing, it's better to do nothing. On the other hand, when you wait for the five stars to line up before you pull the trigger, it may be too late. So you have to find the right happy medium. In order to be three steps ahead of the game, you have to see beyond your eyes. In that way, you can already anticipate the big picture or see the end when only two or three stars are lined up. Like my mother used to say when you wait, "When it begins to smell, then it's too late." That is, you should anticipate what you need to do before it gets too late. For example, you should see a solution for a problem before your competitor or think of obstacles and deal with them in a timely fashion to avoid calamity.

Moving a situation forward may sometimes involve a combination of factors. The key is to remain dynamic and adaptable. This dynamism is directed through your thought. You should think on your feet. Thought is energy in motion. There is hardly a better leverage to change his situation then how you look at it. This is the beginning of the process in moving a situation forward. Remove guesswork from the equation. So summon your desire with persistence and hold the image long enough for the universe to manifest it.

The change of a variable to positively impact a situation may involve self-leadership or putting the unity of vision together in a team. As a soccer coach, I know the individual talent of different players is important. I also know the unity of vision in order to galvanize or focus the individual energies to one big force is crucial for winning. I have to use my dynamism to influence the different players, whether it's through inspiration, motivation, or whatever it takes to chart the course of victory for the team. However, no matter how much I try as a coach, personal dynamism for each player is also important. I find that there's no greater internal motivation than what I call the *dynamic pentad*, the driving forces that spin the wheels of the dynamo. These are:

- The adventurous spirit
- Vision
- A sense of purpose
- Being decisive
- The capacity for growth

These qualities constitute dynamite, and their mastery will turn you into a dynamo. They determine whether you are a high or low performer. These are the levers of leadership. The key to leading is moving a situation forward or creating the result that you want. You start the ball rolling. You create the momentum or upward spiral going. You make the situation right as you get feedback and correct your course once a course of action is initiated. All you need is the technique of affirmation and twenty-one days to instill these qualities into your subconscious mind so their use becomes spontaneous.

For every situation, you have the power of choice to exercise. You can respond with love and compassion or fear and control. This attitude is key to handling any situation, no matter how difficult it is. This is particularly good for a situation where there are no specific solutions. This disposition is key to determining your spiritual and emotional effects of your thoughts. A tough and victorious mental attitude comes with an adventurous spirit. You can then maintain your cool even with fire burning behind you. You can plan for the future, anticipate outcomes, and know how to potentially respond.

Vision is crucial because you need to see the end game. The mind only goes where it perceives. If you do not visualize where you are going to be ten years from now, you will never be there. You will not do what it takes to get there, such as setting appropriate goals, using the right team, and crafting the strategy for success. Having a clear purpose, especially one you deeply believe in, is another great instigator to achieve. This tends to fuel your passion, commitment, and boldness to act.

Curiosity fuels your capacity for growth. Charles Darwin's landmark theory of evolution came from curiosity. He spent time in the woods observing birds and nature. He then coined the expression "survival of the fittest," where animals adapt in order to enhance their nurturing in their respective environment, like the giraffe developing long necks in order to cope.

Having the capacity for growth is important. You have to foster a certain level of independence in your followers. When you have something you stand for, it motivates you to be committed to action. It also helps you develop the can-do attitude that comes with deep belief in yourself and your cause. The question then becomes how to do it and not, if you will. This kind of attitude dissolves any perceived pain or obstacles. You will never know all the facts before making a decision, but you do have to be decisive. Once you decide to act, go for it right now. The fewer facts you have, the more risk you will take.

Taking risk is part of being a leader. If you wait to collect all of the facts, you will always be too late to act. As a leader, you have to stay ahead of the game. You have to see three steps ahead. So put the logic together. When you have two out of five stars lined up, imagine how the end will look. Then pull the trigger when the time is right. Be open and get feedback, reassess the mission, and connect along the way as you go. Make the decision. Watch your timing. Weigh the pros and cons. Feel the adrenaline thumping in your chest. Go with your gut feeling. Pull the trigger.

In this model, decisiveness is crucial. It's the catalyst. Even with all the wisdom and good intentions, nothing happens if you don't act. It's like loading a gun without pulling the trigger. You are motivated and committed, but you have to act in order to create results.

Be dynamic and focused. So you should constantly reassess your options and where you're going. If you do not think ahead and articulate potential obstacles, you would not create a proactive plan and winning strategy. Moment by moment, you should think of what you can do to change the dynamics to move you closer to where you want to be. Use my trademark, Skylimit. Imagination has no limit. Use it to presume that the best things will happen rather than think the worst will. This is how fear and worry is generated. Do not be the circus elephant. It has been overtamed to think in limitations rather than endless possibilities. Look for the factor that will leverage up. Repeated action and momentum keeps the dynamo going.

Your purpose is the big picture or thread that holds everything together. Your purpose or dream transcends your goals or objectives. Goals are the steps you take in order to achieve your purpose. A goal is ongoing pursuit of a worthy purpose until accomplished.

The key question to get to your calling is why you do whatever you are doing. If anything you do does not make a difference, then why do it? You want to feel that you matter or are making a difference on the planet. Self-improvement is an important aspect of guiding yourself in order to succeed. You have to be able to lead yourself or others who are involved in whatever area of success that you desire.

Leading is simply the process of helping yourself or others get somewhere. Ultimately, you have to be able to take care of yourself, even before you try to care for others. You have to be able to deal with challenges by yourself and/or bring in other people or resources to assist you. You are a creative individual, so you should be able to make your own judgments and decisions. The principles outlined here are guidelines on how to face challenges and how to think through problems when they present themselves.

Another way of focusing on your purpose is to ask the simple question, "What are my gifts?" What do you enjoy doing? You can then line up what you do best with a need in the world that you can fulfill. This inevitably gives you a sense of purpose. A sense of purpose makes you feel good about yourself, and it's uplifting. This is the feeling of fulfillment.

How you react to situations depends on your personal philosophy, values, and worldview. Consequently, the information that two billion people live on less than two dollars a day may mean totally different things to different people. This explains why so many people die of hunger on a daily basis.

I always see philanthropy as my calling. Poverty relief is a critical part of it. I want to be the king of philanthropy. I am ready to do anything in my capacity to champion any global initiative that is aimed at relieving poverty. It is no secret that feeding the hungry and getting people educated, especially those without the financial means, are all measures to relieve poverty. There is a very direct correlation between lack of education and poverty. Part of my worldview is that everybody anywhere in the world should have food on the table. It's a basic necessity. In the twenty-first century, people should not die of hunger or go to school hungry.

The greatest hurdle is realizing our dream. I find that people want to start big. The key is to start a positive step. You have to start moving forward in the right direction. Making small, incremental steps each day, like termites gnawing on the root of the tree, is a great secret for success. In the end, the termites are wiser as their seemingly miniature bites fell down a big tree.

My observation and that of people I trust in self-improvement and self-motivation is that a small step taken now is far more important than a giant step articulated later. The only derailment here is determining if the timing is not right. Otherwise, why wait?

Simply identify a niche where there is need for something you are passionate about, like poverty for me. Whatever I do, so long as it's meant to relieve poverty, it lights up my heart. It means I feel fulfilled as my adrenaline is flowing. I then feel energetic as I find that I am acting on purpose.

Always keep in mind what your purpose or dream is. Nimble Jack had a list of his purpose and the goals he wanted to achieve. In that way, he saw them as often as possible. This enabled him to supplant them into his subconscious mind, that is, connect with his basic impulses. He constantly counseled people to visualize their dream life on a daily basis. You simply close your eyes and see your goals complete. This is best done shortly before you go to bed or shortly after getting out of bed in the morning. But any time of the day is good.

If feeding the hungry was your goal, simply see the picture of somebody having a warm meal in your mind's eye. You do not have to prostitute your dream. You can live it very quietly, leaving footprints in a very positive way. I always say you should let others perceive and see their world the way they want it to be. There is a lot of need in the world. We lack people who are prepared to take up these needs as causes to adopt as part of their lives. Do not force people to live the same dream like you. Again, the information here is to help you think through the different steps in order to create and live a dream of your choice. It's not meant to tell you what to think. If you are living a small, insignificant life and not your dream, you are to blame.

Leadership Styles

There are as many leadership styles as there are leaders. Throughout the years, shorthand ways have been developed to describe the main styles. These will help you understand and adapt your styles and impact on your followers.

Whatever your role is, a physician, soccer coach, or leader of a corporation or team at work, your leadership style is crucial to your success. This may essentially happen in a spontaneous fashion. You may not consciously think about it, but, when you analyze your mind-set and behavior, you will realize that you lean toward one of these styles. Understanding these leadership styles and their impact can help you develop and adapt your own leadership style and help you become a more effective leader. These are some of the popular and most talked about leadership styles:

- **Selfless leadership:** I postulated this leadership style. I truly believe that a great leader should have a selfless attitude. This puts the focus where it belongs, positively impacting the world. He or she needs to impart the dynamism explained early in this chapter onto his or her followers or other team players. This manifests into energy and good timing, that is, momentum. To attain this critical mass, repeated victories have to happen. This involves shifting the mind-set of the team members to the creative frequency. To achieve this, he or she has to foster a positive team spirit through motivation, a no-blame policy. This empowers team members to take initiative and risk and be decisive as well. These are all factors that are critical in moving the team forward.

- **Transactional leadership:** This style of leadership starts with the idea that team members agree to obey their leader totally when they take on a job. The "transaction" is usually that the organization pays team members in return for their effort and compliance. The leader has the right to punish team members if their work does not meet the predetermined standard. Team members can do little to improve their job satisfaction under transactional leadership. The leader could give team members some control of their income/reward by using incentives that encourage even higher standards or greater productivity. Alternatively, a transactional leader could practice management by exception. Rather than rewarding better work, he or she would take corrective action if the required standards were not met. Transactional leadership is really just a way of managing rather than a true leadership style, as the focus is on short-term tasks. It has serious limitations for knowledge-based or creative work, but remains a common style in many organizations.

- **Transformational leadership:** A person with this leadership style is a true leader who inspires his or her team constantly with a shared vision of the future. Transformational leaders are highly visible and spend a lot of time communicating. They do not necessarily lead from the front, as they tend to delegate responsibility among their team. While their enthusiasm is often infectious, details people generally need to support them. In many organizations, both transactional and transformational leadership are needed. The transactional leaders or managers ensure that routine work is done reliably while the transformational leaders look after initiatives that add value.

- **Autocratic leadership:** Autocratic leadership is an extreme form of transactional leadership where the leader has absolute power over his or her employees or team. Employees and team members have little opportunity to make suggestions, even if these would be in the team or organization's best interest. Most people tend to resent being treated like this. Because of this, autocratic leaders usually have a hard time retaining followers. When the leadership is forced, the followers are not very willing or productive. For some routine and unskilled jobs, the style can remain effective where the advantages of control outweigh the disadvantages. Bureaucratic leaders work by the book, ensuring their staff follows procedures exactly. This is a very appropriate style for work involving serious safety risks, such as working with machinery, toxic substances, or heights or where large sums of money are involved.

- **Democratic (participative) leadership:** Although a democratic leader will make the final decision, he or she invites other members of the team to contribute to the decision-making process. This not only increases job satisfaction by involving employees or team members in what's going on, but it also helps to develop people's skills. Employees and team members feel in control of their own destiny, such as the promotion they desire. So more than just financial rewards motivate them to work hard. As participation takes time, this approach can lead to things happening more slowly, but the end result is often better. The approach can be most suitable here if the teamwork is essential and quality is more important than speed to market or productivity.

- **Laissez-faire leadership:** This French phrase means "leave it be," and it is used to describe a leader who leaves his or her colleagues to get on with their work. It can be effective if the leader monitors what is being achieved and communicates this back to his or her team regularly. Most often, laissez-faire leadership works for teams in which the individuals are very experienced and skilled self-starters. Unfortunately, it can also refer to situations where managers are not exerting sufficient control.

- **Servant leadership:** This term, coined by Robert Greenleaf in the 1970s, describes a leader who is not formally recognized as such. When someone at any level within an organization leads simply by virtue of meeting the needs of his or her team, he or she is described as a servant leader. In many ways, servant leadership is a form of democratic leadership, as the whole team tends to be involved in decision-making. Supporters of the servant leadership model suggest it is an important way to get ahead in a world where values are increasingly important, in which servant leaders achieve power on the basis of their values and ideals. Others believe that, in competitive leadership situations, people practicing servant leadership will often find themselves left behind by leaders using other leadership styles.

- **Task-oriented leadership:** A highly task-oriented leader focuses only on getting the job done and can be quite autocratic. He or she will actively define the work and roles required, put structures into place, plan, organize, and monitor. However, as task-oriented leaders spare little thought for the well-being of their teams, this approach could suffer many of the flaws of autocratic leadership with difficulties in motivating and retaining staff.

- **People-oriented (relations-oriented) leadership:** The style of leadership is the opposite of task-oriented leadership. The leader is totally focused on organizing, supporting, and developing the people in his or her team. A participative style, it tends to lead to good teamwork and creative collaboration. In practice, most leaders use both task-oriented and people-oriented styles of leadership.

- **Charismatic leadership:** A charismatic leadership style can appear similar to a transformational leadership style in that the leader injects huge doses of enthusiasm into his or her team and is very energetic in driving others forward. However, a charismatic leader tends to believe more in himself or herself than in the team. This can create a risk that a project, even an entire organization, might collapse if the leader were to leave. In the eyes of the followers, success is tied up within the presence of the charismatic leader. As such, charismatic leadership carries great responsibility with it and needs long-term commitment from the leader.

Other Leadership Models

The dynamic model of influence is my preferred model. This comes from the theory that a leader should be like a dynamo. Humans are made up of energy, and we live in a bigger electromagnetic field called the universe. The dynamo therefore is full of energy and passion. In order to be dynamic, he or she has to harness the energy in such a manner as to create the magnetism that is needed to influence, either at an individual or team level.

Moving a situation forward may warrant a combination of factors or leverage. The key is to remain dynamic, thus adaptable and leveraging up. This dynamism is redirected through thought. Thought is energy in motion. This is the beginning of the process in moving a situation forward. You have to summon your desire with persistent thought and hold the image long enough for the universe to manifest. Also instrumental in this model is pulling the trigger decisively when the timing is appropriate. Other leadership approaches may sometimes be more appropriate in a situation or may be used in combination.

A theory attempts to explain why things happen. In my dynamo theory, I have explained what dynamism is and why a leader must be dynamic. A model is a pattern of existing events that can be learned and repeated. In my dynamic model, I have described the pentad step-by-step on how you could become dynamic and stay ahead of the game as well.

An effective leader needs to be a good diagnostician. He or she should also be able to sense and appreciate differences in people and situations. He or she should be adaptable in ways of strategy to succeed, approach, and style to suit the circumstance at hand, like a chameleon. He or she must also know when to use the carrot-and-stick approach. Soft and hard power has their place at the appointed moment. At times, dissent is anticipated and should be quelled promptly before it metastasizes.

Soft power works mainly on the heart through emotional connection and tends to be more effective than hard power, which works on the mind through force. Fighting war at any level is a measure of hard power at its extreme, especially one that is a matter of choice. For George W. Bush, many people still think the avenues of diplomacy and weapons inspections were not thoroughly exploited. Thus, the leader should entertain the possibility of using more than one approach to influence people.

Situational Leadership

You must realize there is no one best way to influence people. Situational leadership is a way of describing and analyzing leadership styles. It is a combination of directive and supportive behavior.

Directive behavior involves telling people what to do, how to do it, where to do it, and when to do it and then closely supervising their performance. Supportive behavior involves listening to people, providing support and encouragement for their efforts, and then facilitating their involvement in problem solving and decision-making.

A situational leader is one who can adapt different leadership styles depending on the situation. Thus, you analyze the needs of the situation and do what is appropriate. This gives them space to grow. I realize that their education compared to mine is a drop in the bucket. In order to strive for a cohesive team spirit, I make them feel appreciated and not chastised. I realize that punishing them for every little thing will instill fear in them and kill their can-do spirit and risk-taking attitude. These qualities are crucial in succeeding in any endeavor. With the space to grow, they feel more comfortable taking measured risk. In this way, they take more responsibility than the average medical assistant would. My assistant sometimes comes up with a problem from the pharmacist, and I challenge her to come up with a solution. I say, "Suppose I was on holiday and you could not reach me? What would you do?" Interestingly, she comes up with the right answer.

The effective leader puts everything on the scale. The level of competence of the follower, the follower's loyalty, and the tools and factors of production needed to move the situation forward are important considerations that any effective leader would consider.

The basis of situational leadership is to provide a means of effective leadership by adopting different leadership styles in different situations with different people. Situational leadership is a model, not a theory. The difference is that a theory attempts to explain why things happen, whereas a model is a pattern of existing events that can be learned and repeated.

Leadership vs. Management

Characteristics of leaders and managers require a combination of the same behavior and skills. For those reasons, there is a lot of overlap between leading and managing. Whatever is said about being a leader or a manager is not exclusive. Individuals basically have to strike a balance between leading and managing.

Leadership focuses more on the why of the mission. It is involved with creating the vision and setting the goals of the project. Depending on the scale of the mission, you may have to train and empower others to understand what the mission is about and help to set goals. This involves developing a culture or relationship for the team or organization, thus the overall picture of the mission.

A manager focuses more on the what and how of the organization, that is, the technical skills for doing and completing the tasks of the project. He directs resources to complete predetermined tasks for the project. He may also have an understanding of the big picture, but he or she focuses on his or her area of interest set by the organization.

In both functions, I think that people's skills are crucial. Building partnerships, creating a team spirit, motivating and empowering employees to focus on their strengths, and taking more responsibility is important.

In my model of dynamic influence, you become a human dynamo to best harness your potential in the same way that we channel energy from the dynamo. Several factors come together in helping accelerate your progress, but drive and motivation are your two horsemen.

VII. Leadership that Lasts

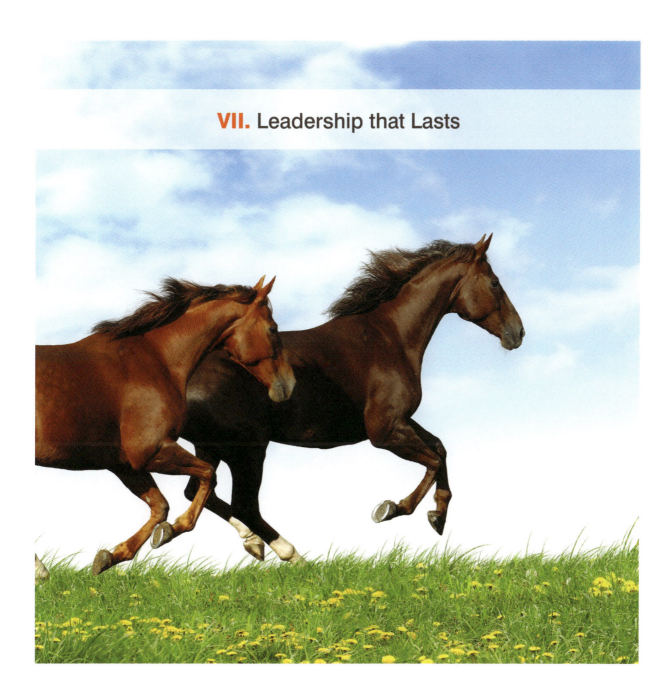

A good leader shares the vision so clearly
that the team can see it also.
The leader then using influence rather than
authority guides them to a successful end.

Ann Marie O'Neill

Chapter Seven

Leadership that Lasts

Winning the Confidence of Those You Lead

Dr. Molly told the story of Mr. Wood. In his words, he was one hell of a buffoon. He was a self-made multimillionaire. He had a lot of authority, but winning the confidence of his followers was not his strength. Dr. Molly says your position may buy you a bit of time, but, in the end, influence is what counts. Eventually, your followers need buy-in. They have to understand the vision. The leader surely charts the course of the vision, but those who follow him or her have to at least have the benefit of doubt. Winning the confidence of those you lead is crucial because it is voluntary process to follow a leader. People decide to follow you based on their own reasons, not yours. Positional leadership has its place, but you sometimes have to follow a leader because of his or her position.

You influence people every day at home at work and in public, in a negative or positive way. Even your silent example may sometimes be more powerful than words.

Many factors are important in creating a following. Dr. Molly asserts that integrity is the first rule of character. Trust is the glue of relationships. If you lack trust, whatever you say is not believable because people do not have faith in you. Character is the bedrock of leadership. You need a strong character in order to succeed.

Mr. Wood waited for too long until he had a calamity on his hands before consulting Dr. Molly for council. He used a checklist of character traits with him. Dr. Molly told Mr. Wood that it is important for him to do a reality check on the leadership qualities that are relevant to his situation. This is sort of like using a mirror to see yourself. In chapter eleven, you can use as many of the leadership qualities as you want on a daily basis for self-improvement. You can actually give yourself a score out of ten for each quality. In that way, you clearly see where your strengths and weaknesses are. This is also being true to yourself. Otherwise, you live in denial. You can then get to practice. Facts are only important when they are put into practice. That's the real art of life mastery. What is the use of a nice thought if it does not become a good deed?

Character traits are supposed to make a change of heart. Learning how to be humble makes you develop a soft heart. This comes out in how you think and relate to people. It makes you also friendlier because you become more open to listen to others as well as learn.

This makes you more successful because most important things are learned by just observing and listening to others speak. This gives your followers more psychological air because people like being listened to. You also become more convincing because you know what people would like. You know how they feel. You know where they stand on an issue. This is a very simple but effective way of being persuasive. People will reciprocate by also listening to you.

Dr. Molly told Mr. Wood to make development of character traits a priority by setting goals on a daily basis in order to improve. He set goals for finding financial achievement. Having a plan for the day makes you focus your energy onto specific tasks that makes you inefficient, so he needed a daily plan to improve his character as well.

Dr. Molly says that, in order to succeed in this exercise, you have to get your true feelings out. You cannot know who you really are if you do not ask yourself questions like:

- Am I happy person?
- Am I a gracious person?

These questions help you focus better on the substance of the matter and not just patting yourself on the back. One of Mr. Wood's problems was that he was very envious. He worked against his competition. He did not like to see anybody else successful in his line of business. He lacked the confidence to be able to stand the thought of seeing someone else succeed. Such is the consequence of taking your eyes off the ball. You dilute your focus. He was so jealous that he lost sight of creating a following that would continue his legacy.

I truly believe that leadership is a great life mastery skill. You need it to be able to draw out benefits from your gifts. This is why I teach success using leadership as a model. It is hard for me to see you move forward without the use of these qualities. They will help you connect with who you are and the external world as well. As a leader, you should be objective enough to be able to sort out your own feelings. You should know what your true feelings are at each moment. You must acknowledge what they are. Otherwise, you would not know how to shift them to where you want to be. Do not deny your true feelings. Rather, acknowledge and release them. Then choose the thought that you want to experience. Why is this important? Emotional stability is very important. For example, when you are out of control or angry, you cannot lead.

There are countless number of ways to show leadership. You can take care of the many disabled children who have no caregivers. Dr. Molly talked about Jamie, who had recently adopted a child from the Children's Aid Society. He said that, even though he had two of his own children, he wanted somebody who could share toys with his children, an experience they otherwise wouldn't have if they had lived in seclusion. Those kinds of things will shape their worldview. They will develop a much wider perspective. Even just fighting over a toy will teach the lesson that life is a bumpy ride. Only experience can teach so many important lessons.

You must learn how to reinvent yourself. Challenges in life are inevitable. They will come. Learn how to pick up the pieces behind you. Get up, dust yourself off, and move on. Mr. Wood learned the affirmation focus and prevailed when one of his companies almost came to bankruptcy. He knew it was more important to consolidate what he had before trying to save the business that was not doing well. Whatever happens, try to always stay upbeat rather than downbeat, as it's a more powerful state of mind to cultivate. It keeps the adrenaline flowing!

A quiet and strong personality reinforces your confidence level. With high self-esteem, you are likely to carry out high-energy conversations. These make you look more like a winner than a loser. It attracts people toward you. This is contrary to the unworthiness that comes from low self-esteem. This lack of mentality makes you feel empty. This is a recipe for a rat race, a destructive competition. When you feel worthy and valuable, disagreeing with people is just natural. You do not lose your cool. This is a more magnetic personality than snapping at people. It makes you much less friendly. You lose your authority and influence.

The ability to sit and wait for the right timing before acting is important. The discipline to get back into the small, calculated steps on a daily basis is important. You need lots of patience for this. Resilience here is also important. It's the ability to get back onto your feet as quickly as possible.

Expect lots of resistance from negative people. It often comes from risk-adverse people, including people who mean well, like family members. You have to be psychologically ready to go against the grain if you want to be successful.

Dr. Molly said that Mr. Wood was too naïve. He got creamed after separation twice with common law partners before he learned his lesson of getting a prenuptial agreement from the lawyer stating that, in case both partners chose to separate, they would go their way just with what they had before coming into the partnership. Agreements like those are signed today, even by people who are to be partners for at least three years. After those number of years, your property gets divided into two. Dr. Molly says that making such an agreement is a reflection of reality because about 50 percent of marriages go up into flames these days. Dr. Molly says this is more important for people who are multimillionaires and do not want to see their property torn apart.

Leadership is hardly a proposition where you add water and stir, but awareness of tried-and-true methods that have moved people to the top of the pack in the world and putting the principles into practice will do you lots of good. As a leader, you would aim for shooting above the top 10 percent of successful people in the world. Simply, push yourself every day out of your comfort zone.

Challenge yourself for doing better, like improving your score on the checklist for your preferred leadership qualities.

It is very important to stay dynamic because people change all the time. People who were good friends or staff members one month ago might have changed their opinion toward you. They may not still be loyal or as honest as they were before. This is why Dr. Molly counsels that you should always conduct yourself as if somebody is watching you. Many things happen when you let your guard down, especially when you do not know who you are dealing with. You hardly have enough time to know everybody or all the negative people out there in the world or even your staff. So your reputation must be maintained. The best way to maintain your credibility is simply do what you do well. The word of mouth goes around, and the spiral of momentum grows. It's more powerful to demonstrate in that sense than try to tell people about yourself.

As the saying goes, "Lead yourself from the head but lead others from the heart." Always make the emotional connection with someone before you ask for his or her help. It works better. Pitch your idea in a persuasive manner and passionately. People like to follow you for their own reasons, but also because you seem comfortable with your own vision. So pitch your idea to the potential prospects with enthusiasm. Also good leaders achieve for themselves and others. People are more energized when they see themselves as part of the vision. They also feel better doing it because they share the vision with you and not just simply because the boss said so. In this way, people do not play the eye servant game on you. They do it when the boss is around. When you are gone, they disappear, too. This makes continuity or sustainability of the mission a problem. Generally speaking, people do not like to do things because they should, but more out of goodwill. You sometimes need to use your authority, like simply telling the teen to either clean up his or her room or be grounded. But using this as a last resort when all the diplomatic avenues have been tried is fair enough.

You have to be like the gods. See the end game. You have to see beyond your eyes. No book will give you all the rules of life mastery, so you need to use your intuition. Always ask yourself why you are not doing your best and what you can do to move forward.

Leadership is more lasting if it is based on influence rather than authority. If you do not aim to be among the top 10 percent of successful people in the world, then you are not thinking big enough.

Don't Be Less Than Your Best.

Angele suggested that her daughter should be prescribed birth control. The only sticky point was that she wanted to trick her daughter into taking it without her knowing what they were. Legally, she deserved to know. Angele wanted to keep it a secret. In her opinion, telling her daughter about the contraception would be like endorsing her sexual activity. This is a complex problem without a simple solution. But knowing how to handle it is key. Here are some guidelines for such issues.

Angele should have stayed as cool as a cucumber. Good leaders are proactive. They anticipate possibilities, negative or positive, and they are never reactive. They wear the hat the moment requires. Accepting things the way they are is being real. It is a great psychological release and frees a lot of your energy. Do no harm to anybody. Angele was harming herself through hysteria. That leads to more worry and stress.

Reconditioning is needed to cement a bedrock of security and confidence. Her actions revealed her own insecurities. When you are concerned enough about a problem, do something about it. You may need to shift your thinking and, consequently, your perception in order to alter your behavior. Knowledge is required to solve problems, so you need to be confident enough to trust your instincts, know your limits, and know when to seek expert opinion. Angele did not recognize the fact that she could not solve this problem without her daughter's cooperation. It's just beyond me how she could have tricked her daughter to take birth control pills without knowing exactly what they are.

Angele is not ready for straight talk with her daughter. She ought to be principled-centered. She was too family-centered, and it blurred her perception of other realities, like the fact that her daughter needed to grow in many areas, including making her own decisions and becoming accountable for her actions.

The attitude of overprotecting and providing everything to people stifles creativity and fosters a lack of initiative and dependency, too. Encouragement, support, and straight talk are important developmental boosters. But I cannot emphasize enough the fact that most personal growth and strength are rooted within. The turning point comes when you take accountability for your actions. Only you can summon whatever you want through your feelings and thoughts.

Finally, brainstorm for practical solutions. The problem-solution model is good. Frame the problem into a question. Then write down as many options as you can. Have a simple, strategic plan, and be realistic about what you can do. You simply cannot change some things. But always remember that attitude is more powerful than facts.

We are all born for a common purpose, to serve God. The Bible says you should show your love by feeding his sheep. Filling up your pockets with money is inadequate service because you are missing the utmost mark, service for God. It's the primary motive for what you do. Your career is not more than a means to serve God. What use is it if whatever you do does not positively impact that society? This is the real measure of a man making a difference in people's lives. It's very important because people could sing the same song yet dance totally differently.

Living on purpose is what creates happiness. The daily activities and struggles of life bring victories and happiness. It's going to bed knowing you fed one of God's children today that puts a smile on your face. It's the highest calling for you as you walk the earth. In the end, the nature of the service does not matter. It only matters that it serves the primary purpose, which is to positively impact your world.

You must always remember that both good and evil exist, just in the same way that light and darkness exist.

One day, the scorpion and frog arrived simultaneously at the riverbank. They were about to cross to the opposite side. The scorpion didn't know how to swim, so he asked for the frog to give him a ride on his back across the river. The frog agreed. Halfway across, the scorpion stung the frog. As they both were drowning, the frog asked the scorpion why he did that. "Because I am a scorpion," the scorpion replied. The frog was too naïve. He failed to recognize the scorpion for what he was and lost the battle of good and evil that is always on. Conventional thinking is not always right.

Grasp the gravity of the situation, and contemplate a measured response. You can only do this when you are quiet and relaxed. Sometimes, the best thing to do is nothing. What you do not do in a situation is sometimes just as powerful as when you do something.

As you think about it, how many bullets were fired before the Cold War between Russia and the West ended? Diplomacy, not bullets, brought down the Berlin Wall. More than half the game of diplomacy is what you do not do. My mother's motto is, "Always say less than necessary." She thinks there are no neutral words.

Inductive thinkers observe facts before forming a theory. But, in deductive thinking, people form a theory before they observe the facts to support it. The slippery slope with deductive thinking is that you are more likely to not only be subjective, but personalize the situation. People weigh in before taking sides. Consequently, they are standoffish.

Create the magnetic effect of connection. Self-control with the dignified pose is important. Never argue because it is a show of weakness. Staying in touch with your basic impulses by staying quiet and relaxed is very powerful. Like attracts like. Seeking common ground is what initiates positive energy that moves your momentum forward. Charisma is more important than charm, but they are both seductive. My friend Oscar observed that a few powerful words with the right timing are more important than preaching.

The Power of Focus

Knowing how to focus is your first rule of success. Activity is not necessarily accomplishment. Long-term planning and prioritizing makes you see ahead what you are supposed to do. In that way, you can be proactive, making time for important tasks. It makes you less reactive. I like the maxim, "A stitch in time saves nine." In your life, you will tailor your actions to align with your values.

Termites and bees are very powerful creatures. We can learn a lot from them. Their secret is the small steps on a daily basis, the plodding along. Their subtlety is very effective. The Bible puts it this way, "Four things on earth are extremely wise: ants are creatures of little strength, yet they store up their food in the summer."[21]

I never do anything that my assistants can do. I always figure out what I must do, even if I can do it. I also make sure that the activity catches my heart, not just my eye.

Good leaders seek out what brings the greatest return. They also analyze their followers and themselves to figure out what their strengths and weaknesses are. If you do not study your staff, you will not create a leadership pipe that matches aptitude with strategy. In that way, you are doomed to fail.

It has been repeatedly shown that one or two big ideas with one general theme work better than many disjointed plans. I have already explained how to shift your attention onto the task at hand or whatever you want to experience. Use oppositional thinking. Take calculated risks. If Winston Churchill did not make victory his goal, we would have been living in Adolf Hitler's world today. Who knows what that would have been like?

So always ask yourself what you really want to get out of life when you create your heroic mission. It is the central piece of your philosophy. It is your mirror, so you can compare yourself with it every day and see how much progress or lack thereof that you are making.

Good leaders stay well grounded, both physically and psychologically. You have to be constantly seeking renewal and know how to unwind. Your internal dialogue determines who and what you become. Pep yourself, but more from philosophical refinement to being a doer by just learning to do things rather

---

21   Proverbs 30:24-25

than talk too much about them. Look for those activities that bring you the greatest reward or fulfillment.

Be a straight shooter. Direct and straight talk is a great time-saver. Communication is about emphasizing what is important. Terse sound bites are very effective. Muffled communication and rambling are not.

The easiest way to overshoot is to be bombastic. Nothing is ever right when you are dealing with a cynic. They see the way it should be, not the way it is, so use subtlety in order to be effective here. In this case, a few well-timed words are more effective than rambling. It pushes you to focus on the essence and makes you articulate better, so it is a more powerful means of communication.

Also use the 20-80 rule. Focus on the top 20 percent of your action list. It's about concentrating on your top priorities. It gives you 80 percent of your productivity. You can then delegate the rest. If the rest of your activities do not catch your heart, you can look for a new number one on your action list.

Another important principle for prioritizing is that you have to create time for important activities. Cultivate the action habit. Match your actions with your intentions.

Build an execution culture in your organization. Attach benchmarks of excellence to the rewards for your staff. Motivation and blameless culture are good drivers of excellence. In such a culture, people feel empowered, making them take more risk and responsibility, which fosters creativity and innovation. You will never spend enough time training staff. It's the way to multiply your impact. Also put the right people in the right places.

Surveys show that having one big idea with a general theme that you can tap into often works better than too many disjointed ideas. It's the law of concentration. Don't dissipate your energy.

Great leaders know how to create excitement and enthusiasm. It greatly enhances team chemistry. You can also improve your results with the law of averages. If you do something long enough, you get a ratio of results. If you hear no too many times at the start of your plodding, trying repeatedly will get people to say yes. Instincts and intuition is needed. Review your heroic mission every day. Be the mirror to your world. This refocuses you on what is important. Toss your heroic mission into your subconscious mind all day. Thinking, planning ahead, and being obsessed in your heroic mission enhance your focus. Stay on task by using oppositional thinking and gratitude for any accomplishment obtained.

VIII. Better Health with Self-Leadership

Happier thoughts lead to a happier chemistry. A happier, healthier body. Negative thoughts and stress have been shown to seriously degrade the body and the functioning of the brain because it's our thoughts and emotions that are continuously reassembling, reorganizing and recreating our body.

Dr. John Hagelin

Chapter Eight

Better Health with Self-leadership

Wellness and Weight Control

You can set a simple health goal, like keeping an ideal weight. It is one of the greatest challenges of health maintenance. The health benefits related to ideal weight management are staggering. Obesity is one of the major risk factors for both morbidity and disease causation. Having a goal to keep fit motivates you and gives you something to shoot for. You have to practice until you assimilate the goal into your lifestyle.

Weight management will positively influence your health status. Even in a very implicit fashion, whatever you do to move forward often involves some form of leadership. You may not call it as such, but it is. This often involves taking positive steps toward whatever you want to achieve. You have to actively do something. Otherwise, all of the positive attitude we have talked about will not do the action.

Being overweight or unfit increases your risk of common killers, like diabetes, heart attack, stroke, anxiety, and cancer. Half of the deaths in North America are due to heart problems. Follow a healthy eating and exercise plan to reduce your risk for these common conditions. To best prevent them, you can live as if you have them. The rationale for this mind-set is that, when you wait until you are diagnosed with the ailment, it's too late to prevent it.

Healthy eating and exercise reduce your cholesterol and blood sugar levels. They also increase your serotonin level.

Exercise

Adopt daily exercise regimens that are tailored to your needs. For weight management and cardiac fitness, breathing exercises increase oxygen supply to your body, especially the brain. The serotonin levels also pop up. Very simple actions like walking or jogging for thirty minutes each day can make you lose ounces every day. But this compounds over time to pounds. Another great tip is to start your dinner with salads and fruits because they are lighter than meat. Eat more fruits and vegetables, as they are rich in potassium, which gives your muscles more tone and you more energy.

Regular exercise, meditation, and yoga are antidotes to stress. High stress increases your cortisol level, which further increases your chance for diabetes and high blood pressure. Exercise is essential to good health. Stressors are things that can either trigger disease or make you stressed out. These could be physical or psychological in nature. They are mostly life events like job loss, loss of a partner, diagnosis with a disease, or even a perceived loss. These triggers can cause psychological stress that may lead to psychosomatic problems, such as headaches, fatigue, and so forth.

The key to adding exercise to your lifestyle is to choose something you enjoy. About thirty minutes of walking, rowing, swimming, or bike riding four to seven days a week is ideal. This could lead to shedding off about one thousand calories per week off your weight. A good rule of thumb is to exercise until you are sweating (sweat test). Cross training (walking and rowing every other day) gives you variety and a way to avoid injury. Exercise is a positive distraction from worries. It increases your energy and enthusiasm. Exercising regularly strengthens your heart and helps you manage your weight, blood sugar, cholesterol level, and blood pressure.

Rest

Lack of rest increases both your stress and cortisol levels, which, in turn, increase your chances for developing diabetes. In order to perform well, think clearly, and make good decisions, a proper amount of rest is vital.

Positive Mental Attitude

With a positive mental attitude, you are still real because you recognize the problem or potential failure. You simply choose not to dwell on it. Use your creativity to break the habit of worry. Anxiety, stress, and hurry are the number-one killers in our world. Realize that sorrow comes to everyone. Learn how to meet it the same as others. The sufferer must avoid the temptation to brood. Everything is created twice. The blueprint in the mind represents the internal dialogue. This then affects our perception and external dialogue. Brooding imposes a lot of mental pain. It's a vicious cycle that stokes a negative internal dialogue: insecurity, procrastination, and melancholia.

Use meaningful escapism. Go through the grieving process rather than deny it. Survival of soul in the next world makes death not a barrier. The Bible promises comfort, immortality and reunion, and every good thing to those who center their lives in God. "No eye has seen, no ear has heard, no mind has conceived what God has prepared for those who love Him." [22]

God is the greatest healer by any measurement you use. He conquered death himself through the Resurrection, soul over matter. He raised the dead and cured people of incurable diseases. "Take heart, daughter, he said, your faith has healed you. And the woman was healed from that moment."[23]

Yearly checkups with your physician are also an important component of health maintenance. It is more important to be aware of risk factors that cause heart disease and avoid them rather than wait until you have a heart attack. An early

22   Corinthians 2:9
23   Corinthians 2:9

diagnosis is always preferable to a late one because you have a better chance of cure.

The Power Formula

Never be the victim of adversity. We should instead draw upon the higher power. This is done simply through practicing the Bible. Quiet yourself through meditation and prayer. Relax. Practice resting by yielding yourself to God. In this way, you depend upon him for his support and power. Believe you are a vessel through which God is acting. If you truly believe that he is giving to you now, then you are yielding and letting the Holy Spirit make the connection by flowing through you. With this cavalier and nonchalant approach, you see the end and do your best without fretting for the outcome.

"Those who hope in the Lord will renew their strength." [24]God is our source. He never fails anybody. All the strength and hope you need, God will give to you. All you need to do is ask, like King Solomon. "According to your faith, it will be done to you."[25] This is a basic law of successful living. According to your faith presupposes in proportion to your faith. Cultivate the habit of taking a positive, optimistic attitude toward every problem. In direct proportion to the intensity of your faith, you will receive power to meet your situation.

Gain power over your difficulties through God's help. Never feel too sophisticated to permit the Lord to do his great work through you through trust and faith. He is a great healer. No one knows better than him. Hope and faith are selfless, and so is leadership. Shifting the balance of power to God's favor is to your advantage. It rids you of the burden of responsibility when you know that he is the source and things are done through you, but you are not the object.

We all need a day-to-day job on ourselves of reviewing the wealth of wisdom in the Bible and trying to put it into practice. It is the greatest formula for becoming more powerful and authentic as we begin to live a more radiant lifestyle. So adopting the power formula will empower our character as well.

---

24   Mathew 9:29
25   . Mathew 9:22

The image of the sun is very powerful. It represents the light, that is, virtue. Adopt this powerful image where the fruits of the spirit and all things good, humble, confident, wise, hopeful and come from.

Use some of the practical techniques in chapter three regarding meditation and visualization. Use the oppositional thinking method to supplant ideas that you deem worthy. This is a good technique for rehearsing your blueprint and reconditioning your mind.

Model enthusiasm that ignites passion, especially when the fuel of a noble cause is present. Use the think-act-feel triad to cultivate any of the qualities that would lead to self-improvement for you.

Learn to be humble but not timid. Be brave and confident, but not fearful. Learn to express, not impress. Some people operate from a perspective of false humility. These people believe the myth that you need to worry about things to prove that you care. Here is my take. If you care enough about something, then do something about it. Do not waste time worrying about it. It is like outsourcing your energy or short-circuiting, where electrical power is wasted as resistance rather than harnessing it for consumption as light.

IX. The Psychology of Winning

You create your own universe as you go along.

Winston Churchill

Chapter Nine

The Psychology of Winning

Thinking Like a Winner

Surely learning how to stand on the shoulders of giants is important, but you can only create what you summon with your feelings and thoughts, not what your friend or parents want you to become. Humility enables us to learn from other people's mistakes. That is very important as you can never live long enough to learn or discover everything by yourself.

A cardinal rule of success is to believe in yourself. Belief, like fear, is a very powerful influence. Simply, you must become what you believe and think about daily. So your own self-image will determine whether you succeed or fail. No wonder Emerson said you are what you think all day long. Your internal dialogue determines who you are and, eventually, what you become.

One reason for believing in yourself is that no one wants to follow an insecure leader. You have to think like a leader in order to sound like one. You are measured by the words you use. Feeling secure and confident and sounding like a star is important. Style almost always wins over substance. The truth is not in the evidence, but it's in the way you think.

As a leader, you need to think on your feet. You have to be spontaneous. Life is about solving problems. Make sure that 90 percent of your time is spent on finding the solution. Spend enough time on the problem, just to define and understand it. Use the rest of your time concentrating your energy on solving it.

Affirmations are proven concepts that work. Simply state that it is already so. See in your mind's eye where you want to be. Create quotes or pictures of your blueprint so you can look at them every day. Ruthie, my daughter, drew a picture of a house for me. At the time, I was planning to start a bank, so I colored it with a "B" on it, which meant "bank" to me. This picture is still hanging on the wall in my office. Looking at it every day certainly stokes my passion of transforming my idea into reality.

When you believe in what you stand for, do not listen to the prophets of doom. The only question is whether what you want to do is consistent with your values or not. Avoid negative people who throw a grenade onto your ideas.

You have to be effective in self-promotion. You have to believe in it and be passionate about it. You also have to be assertive about it. When I pitch my vision for the charitable foundation, I do not need to think about it because its vision is part of my moral fiber. It takes seconds to sell a vision that you believe in.

Selling is very important. If you do not sell, people don't know about your vision. For Skylimit Corporation, we put ads in the newspaper and on television and sent flyers around. As you think about it, if you do not promote your service or skill, people will not know about it. You cannot produce results, which is the name of the game of success.

When I started my own clinic, I felt more energized and passionate, even elated, about work. Unquestionably, in my mind, I felt this was my own creation so I connected more with it to my heart. I felt victorious as well. Having my own clinic put an end to going to look for work in other clinics in town. This thought also freed my energy.

A good leader will never allow sadness to overwhelm him or her. An attitude of confidence and optimism can work miracles. Being optimistic and expecting the best can make all the difference.

One of the keys to becoming a winner is to always picture success in your mind, no matter how bad things are. Worrying will not make a positive difference. In the end, you have to find your voice and stand for it.

As a leader, your motto should be victory. You should never consider failure as a possibility, but, likewise, you should never be afraid of failing. I know so many people who see setbacks as stepping-stones. A good leader will accept the fact that failure occurs, accept responsibility for it, and move on to something positive.

As a physician, I make great use of some of the problem-solving techniques described previously. So I often frame whatever issue I have as a question, think about the solutions or answers, and write down as many as I can. I run through the list and come up with the best answer for any given situation. I often say that being a good diagnostician is like being a gold digger. You only dig where you think you might find gold. So you elicit the kind of questions that will lead to your diagnosis. Observation is sometimes the best way to figure out what is wrong. It is useful in life as well. If you anticipate what you might find, you focus better. You only see what you look for. If you do not think of the different options, you won't see the big picture.

Our first fund-raiser for the Nkut Foundation was focused on a famous Christian comedian singer/songwriter named Mark Lowry who recorded the famous Christian hit song, "Mary, Did You Know?" The song had gained massive airplay after it appeared in Mel Gibson's film, *The Passion. American Idol* finalist Clay Aiken, Kenny Rogers, Wynonna Judd, and Rascal Flatts also recorded it. The fund-raiser was a no-brainer as far as entertainment was concerned. Mark Lowry had now reached the peak of his career. Coincidentally, it coincided with the beginning of our first campaign.

The success of the concert enabled the Nkut Foundation to donate profits to a local soup kitchen and homeless shelter, giving the foundation credibility and making it a force to be reckoned with. With the attitude of "go big or go home," we jumped into our second fund-raiser by securing a date with one of America's number-one selling bands from the 1980s.

Unfortunately, due to the excitement over the success of our first show, we did not exercise patience. Even though the show was done to professional standards and all parties were taken care of, the concert flopped due to poor ticket sales. We recognized that starting from the beginning and climbing the business ladder takes time and patience.

Once again, it's not what happened to you. It's how you handled it. It's not where you have been. It's where you are going. It's also the determination and discipline to do it. When willed, it's half-done, said Abraham Lincoln.[26]

Strategic intention is important. You have to be a great visionary. Know where you want to be many years down the road because you cannot plan ahead until you do. Start renaming your experiences. The winner can see an opportunity in even those situations that the mediocre people see as a crisis. Embrace controversy. Just to put it bluntly, it sells!

Acting Like a Winner

If you were to cultivate one habit, action should be it. It is the single-most important habit that will move you to the top. You can dither along with lots of knowledge, but what makes the difference is what you do.

A step you take today, no matter how small, is better than a giant step anticipated years down the road. If you are thinking of doing anything tomorrow, for example, write a book, why not start today? Only you are holding yourself back. So long as you are interested in writing on that subject, the brainstorming and research will be fulfilling. Once you start, you have made a commitment. Your conscious mind has put the subconscious mind to work for you. It is the command center, the camera. The subconscious in harmony with the universal intelligence will aid you in the process of solving the problem or writing the book.

If you are really interested in the subject, your heart will get charged up, and you become passionate about it. This gives you the momentum to keep going. If the project is really a priority or a dream that you want to see realized, you will make time for it. You can initiate research or do interviews with people who know the material that you need for your book or project in question.

---

26   Barny Sears, *The Zone.*

This is a basic principle that works miracles. If you ever wait to know everything before you start a new project, you will never do anything. This is why perfectionists do not do much. They wait until they know it all, which is impossible. They leave the house and wait for all the lights to turn green before they go where they want to go. It is a small wonder that they never reach their destination. While they are waiting for all the lights to turn green, they procrastinate and brood and become hysterical and melancholic. It's such a vicious cycle. Rather than live one day at a time, they run their whole life in front of them like a movie. That can be very overwhelming to do.

For the winners, when one light turns green, they proceed through, taking one step at a time. When they come to a red light, they use their imagination and visualize and connect with what they could be, not only on what is. The red light does not frustrate them. They are part of the process. Challenges are the crux of adventure. They energize you and set you on fire. Life is about solving problems. That process keeps you going and passionate. You have to have a dog in the bone of life! Otherwise, life is flat.

Winners are often passionate, charismatic, and energetic, so they charge ahead through tasks without giving it much thought. They just have fun swinging the bat. Even if it hurts them, they know it is part of the process, and they do not retreat. You see that attitudes are more important than facts.

Nimble Jack learned how to dress and act his part. Many years of coaching turned him into a high achiever. The crisis of separation with his wife did him some good, too. It drew him out of his comfort zone. Jack confided in Dr. Molly that he was initially afraid, but, when he sat down and brainstormed, he realized nobody else could do it for him.

Selling and Negotiating

Marketing and selling skills are very important. You can create the greatest product or have the greatest qualities as a leader, but you cannot move ahead if you cannot sell them. When you set a vision, people ask themselves, "Does this leader really mean what he promised?" The second (and even more important question) is, "Does he have my best interest at heart?" People do things for their own reasons, not yours.

Oscar Gionet, a board member at the Nkut Foundation, is an emotionalist. He sees beyond his eyes. He always emphasizes that the point is all about giving. Everyone on the board ought to be comfortable with the idea. He says we should only attract people who are willing to give of themselves and their resources. I agree with him because we are cultivating the leadership culture in this organization where the focus is giving to the poor. Such leaders analyze the needs of the poor and see where we can help, not allow themselves to be preoccupied with their own insecurity and ego.

Oscar maintains that the only way to do this is not to try to convince people to join the organization. Our pitch to friends and well-wishers should be convincing. The best way to bring somebody to your side is to connect with him or her by making your sales pitch. If he or she believes in you, the leader, and the vision, he or she will join you. It's far better than putting pressure on somebody who may join against his or her will, pay lip service, become cynical, and criticize rather than look out for the needs of the organization to advance the cause it set out for.

Experts can do this for you, too. When Lynn and I got the television involved with marketing for Skylimit Corporation, we noticed a very quick rise in profits. At first, we depended just on word of mouth, but we realized we needed to reach a bigger population. Having a picture in your mind of what is acceptable for you is important.

People skills are crucial in negotiating deals. Keep the options open, listen, and read the person with whom you are dealing. In making deals, remember you have a great deal to offer and the other person is going to be benefit just as much as you, if not more. When you are negotiating a deal, you are selling an idea, yourself, or something else of value.

Acting casually and not showing a lot of interest disarms your opponent. Don't be like the Pentecostal preacher. Stay in touch with your impulses. Think on your feet. Always say to yourself, "What's the hidden cost here?" Does this sound too good to be true? When somebody hints at quick closure or brings in an element of hurry, back off a little bit.

It is best to stay calm and levelheaded when negotiating. Just the thought of doing something worthy, both for yourself and people who may share in some of your observations about life, adds value to everybody, uplifts you, and reinforces your positive mental attitude. You will start thinking in terms of now or tomorrow rather than yesterday.

Always think about loose ends to tie up before closure. These may be anything, including the legal end of things. Even when you do not entirely agree on a deal, it's good to end with a high positive note. It tweaks the brain positively. You could do this formally or informally. Use any tactic that works for you.

If you are not too sure, you may put an escape clause on a deal without voicing this to your opponent. You can say something like "subject to availability of finances" or even your wife's approval, depending on the circumstances.

The Litmus Test for Leadership

Make that paradigm shift. Begin living by design and not default. Your world is the result of your thoughts, the cause of all meaningful outcomes. Only through acting you can summon what you want through your subconscious from your universal intelligence. Nobody else can do it for you.

Why are you not among the top 10 percent of the most successful people in the world? Leaders do not make a living. They make a life. They shoot to the top of Maslow's pyramid for self-actualization. Decide now to go after the rest of your potentials. Maslow said, "What a man can be must be." What sort of worldview or legacy are you interested in? You change the world by one act of love at a time. Focus on your priorities, but, above all, cultivate the habit of feeling secure, open-minded, successful, happy, loving, curious, and ambitious. These crucial components drive creativity, growth, and the process.

Unquestionably, the long-held tradition in the world of psychology that attitudes are more powerful than facts is still true. The mind can magnify or minimize objects depending on your state of mind. Two people can face the same dilemma with two totally opposing viewpoints. The primary difference must reside on the way they think, not the facts. Of course, facts are important. To connect with somebody, you need to draw him or her in emotionally. But that's not enough sometimes. You need to show that you can produce results or deliver. Actions speak louder than words.

According to the mind principle already discussed, you really do not possess anything physically, except in your own consciousness. Again, it is the belief that produces the results, not what you believe in. Belief is the object. What you believe is the subject. Your thoughts are modeled according to your beliefs, so the results are effects.

The degree of attachment to anything depends on your state of mind and the value you assign to the thing. If you have seen a patient with severe dementia either in the nursing home or hospital, you will understand what I mean. But let me explain. People with this condition do not even recognize their family members. This can be very upsetting for those family members.

Positive thinking is a form of thought process that habitually looks for the best results in even seemingly dire situations. It is always possible to look for something positive to build on. Your psychology has a powerful effect in getting your physiology on board to get the adrenaline flowing. It keeps your passion, momentum, energy, and dynamism buzzing.

The fact is that, when you seek good, you are likely to find it. Positive thinking is a deliberate process and matter of choice. Lincoln said that most people could be as happy as they wish to be.

Nimble Jack took the hunger test. It puts you in touch with your basic instincts, and the spiritual benefit of it can spread to other areas of your life. It refocuses you to whatever you want. Nimble Jack started fasting for five days. He became hungry for food. In his words, he assigned a totally different value for food.

When you really want to achieve success, you will re-create the hunger experience. This puts you in touch with your basic impulses. Whatever you want as much as you wanted (for example, food after five days of fasting), you will receive it.

This very powerful technique toughens and reconditions your mind for success. To think right is to create your own experience. You eventually become what you feel and think. When you have the hunger or desire for anything, you come to the clear decision that there is no way out. Victory is assumed.

This experience awakens your infinite mental and spiritual powers. Once you cultivate the habit to identify your thoughts with your heroic mission in life, you cease to become upset by people. The secret then is to precondition your mind to successful living. Create a blueprint that reflects what success means to you. Use the practical techniques described in chapter three.

Success is handling your life effectively and efficiently. It means to be controlled, generous, gracious, happy, and positively impacting the world. You can see why this book was started on the heroic mission. It's more than a purpose or a goal. It encompasses the legacy and reason behind the reason.

You can only achieve that which you conceive of. Your heroic mission is crucial. Also, make sure it is in harmony with God's desire for you. Material success alone is not success. Abundance in all areas is important.

Success for the leader also means taking his or her team or organization to where it wants to go. The best recipe is the one that works for you. Regardless of your belief system, you can quiet your mind by using the practical techniques in this book. The quiet state when you are calm and cool is when your mind is most creative. You cannot think straight if your mind is not quiet or still. Some people use prayer, meditation, or yoga. The common denominator is that these are all forms of focused thinking.

You can be your own coach as you commit to daily growth and excellence. Strategically position yourself to influence other people by improving on those core competencies that will make you more effective and efficient. Look at the figure that shows you the six core competencies.

Nimble Jack became the success master. He lives by design, not default. The best of him is yet to come because he has not peaked yet. He has espoused the go-big-or-go-home attitude. Not only did my message resonate, it captured his imagination as well. He truly believes that, in life, there are no limits but the sky. He is determined to succeed despite the obstacles thrown onto his path.

X. Good to Great

The true value of a person is measured by the following criteria: integrity, generosity, graciousness, and contribution to the general good.

Denis Waitley

Chapter Ten

Good to Great

Remember Denis Waitley's words. Life itself is a treasure, not a treasure hunt. When gratitude is your way of life, you count your blessings, not losses. You choose to talk about the good, not the bad. You stop being cynical. When you smile, you stimulate the body to produce endorphins, and these chemicals make you feel happy. Cynics analyze and criticize rather than focus on the needs of the situation. That negative mind-set makes them see the worst rather than the best in themselves and in others. Be one of those who leap from mediocrity to greatness. Hardly anything will move you forward more powerfully than the servant attitude. How can I serve you?

So many powerful character traits that are important in the success process come from grace: the attitude of gratitude, service, and selflessness and the spirit of abundance. Grace means free favor from our God shown toward man; gratitude is the feeling of being thankful or appreciative. Gratitude is also being grateful no matter where you are and no matter what your circumstance is, failure or success. Wherever you are in your quest for success, be happy!

We are supposed to follow this example of generosity toward other people. In that way, we become graceful as we serve out of love. We expect nothing in return. When we serve or give with the expectation of getting something in return, it's called trading. In that way, giving is loss, not gain. We also feel that, in order to get, we take rather than give. True generosity is when you believe that giving is receiving, that is, is love, so you put out love in the universe automatically. You give without thinking. Giving energizes you as you also feel even more blessed giving than receiving. You know that things are coming through you, not from you. You become selfless or humble because you see yourself as a vehicle for positively impacting other people's lives. This is where your abundant mentality also comes from because you sense that the source is infinite.

Rhonda Byrne, in *The Secret*, asserts that gratitude is so powerful that it could be seen as a law. She thinks this is an important streak that should be practiced until it becomes a way of life.[27]

Gratitude is positive energy. It magnetizes and draws you closer into the feeling good, creative frequency. The end result is then success as the universe releases or manifests what you summon through your thoughts and feelings, that is, the Law of Attraction. Abundance in all areas of your life is yours.

Zig Ziggler, author and motivational speaker, put it this way. If you help enough people get what they want, you will eventually get what you want! The way to heaven is by helping others, not hurting them.[28] Remember the words of the lord Jesus. He himself said, "It is more blessed to give than to receive."[29] Few areas of our lives can be more fulfilling than the area of giving. Throughout the Bible, we are encouraged to be generous and to give. Numerous passages in the Bible deal with this important subject of giving.

You may remember the story of the poor widow who gave everything she had to the church. This attitude in giving is what Jesus emphasizes most. "If I give all my possessions to feed the poor, but have not love; it profits me in no way."[30] Thus, if a gift is given with the proper attitude of love and service, then the giver benefits more than the receiver.

---

27   Rhonda Byrne, The Secret
28   Zig Ziggler; The Secret to Millionaire Success
29   Acts 20:35
30   Corinthians 13:3

God set the example of giving motivated by love. "For God so loves the world, he gave his only begotten son, that whosoever believed in him shall not parish, but live in an everlasting life."[31]

Charity is a good word. Its roots are in the Latin word for "affection" and "dear." It's used to describe an action, a generous gesture motivated by genuine affection and caring.

Since 1950, the word *charity* has been personified by the actions of the missionaries of charity. Beginning with twelve workers in Calcutta, today there are about five thousand all over the world, continuing the work of Mother Teresa. In her own words, her work constituted of caring for the hungry, homeless, crippled, and all those people who feel unloved and unwanted.

Mother Teresa and her missionaries were willing to go looking for ways to extend the love of God. They did not sit back and wait for the needy to come to them. They went out into the streets of the world's largest cities, found those who have been shunned by everyone, and brought them in to meet their needs. That is the true heart of charity, love.

God did not wait for the human race to come to him for help. He sent forth his son into the world to seek out and save that which was lost.[32] The story of the Good Samaritan is as good a human illustration of charity as you will ever find. Before the Good Samaritan encountered the man who had been attacked, robbed, and left for dead, two others had passed by and done nothing. But the Good Samaritan crossed the road and extended love and compassion. He bandaged the man, took him to an inn, and paid for his room and board while he recovered. He could not do everything, but he did what he could. Having gratitude for your followers and colleagues in helping you achieve your vision will result in their increased desire to help you. Having gratitude for all the events of your life that helped you get to this point will give you a desire to make the most of what you have. It will also help you realize that you can help others get where they want to be just as you were helped in getting where you are.

---

31   John 3:16
32   Malachi 3:18

Service is the highest calling that there is. We should be serving the kingdom. Remember the parable of the vineyard where Jesus told the disciple that he is the vine and they are the branches. And they cannot do anything without him. Just like the branches of the vine cannot bear fruit without the tree.[33] Serve God with all the capital you have: spiritual, ideas, money, talents, skills, gifts, and your time. Use your resources in eternally significant ways. This is the only way you can use your resources to secure an eternal resting place for yourself in the next world. This is because only your soul moves to the next world.

Having the right attitude is the key here. Knowing God is in the ultimate control of everything is crucial. "The earth is the Lord's and all it contains."[34] If we would heed to this basic awareness that God is the owner of everything, it will dissolve a lot of the suffocating materialism that robs many of us of spiritual vitality.

The Bible has answers to most financial difficulties that the world faces. Surveys reveal that more than half of all divorces are a result of financial tension in the home. "But lay up for yourselves treasures in heaven."[35] "There is one who scatters, yet increases all the more and there is one who withholds what is justly due, but it results in want. The generous man will be prosperous, and he who waters will himself be watered."[36]

The Bible also says that, what you do for the least of us, you do it for God. Doing even your work with gratitude makes it more fulfilling. Lacking the passion to do what you do leads to boredom and frustration. Begin to work with gratitude. Pep up yourself for serving a need and contributing to the service of the kingdom. Service is the highest calling there is. You can create satisfaction from your work. Scripture does not elevate any honest profession above another. "Whatever you do, do your work heartily, as of the Lord rather than for men ... It's the lord Christ when you serve."[37]

33	Luke 19:10
34	John 15:1
35	Psalm 24:1
36	Mathew 6:20
37	Proverbs 11:24

We are encouraged to be like the ants. Their steady plodding brings prosperity. God knows you have to keep earning to keep giving. There is a connection. Rewards are linked with service, as in the story of Jesus encouraging the servant who used his money to make more and chided the servant who buried his money in the ground.

Meditate and pray for gratitude, too. God is both predictable and unpredictable. He has an endless number of ways to bless us. Our prayers are answered. It may be in a way that we do not understand because we can never outdo God in gratitude or anything else. Honor God with your tithing. He will then trust you and give you more, but in ways you may not recognize.

Aristotle held to the view that basic laws guide life. He observed that the common theme uniting the greatest leaders is caring for others. To move to the perfection of our nature, we start by helping others. That is what gets us to heaven as well. So gratitude is the gateway into your next world. It's so powerful that it could be seen as a law.

Charity begins at home, so the best place to start is where you are. Thinking is so powerful that, in order to change your current circumstances, you have to first change your thinking. No wonder Buddha noted that all you are is a result of your thoughts. It begins with sowing a thought of gratitude. A deed of gratitude follows, and an act of gratitude follows, too.

Gratitude begins with feeling grateful about your current circumstances, whatever is happening. This simple thought tips your thought energy to the creative frequency, the feeling of good energy. Thoughts are things. They are energy in motion. Say thank you and feel gracious until the habit of giving rather than taking becomes second nature. This is when it becomes a way of life.

Bob Proctor talks about reaching the stage of unconscious competence, where you think that it's God or the universe delivering the money or service through you. At that point, you do not hold back giving in any form, including service, praise, mercy, grace, loving, and even being just appreciative. Gratitude brings order to your life.

In order to attract things or people that are positive, you have to be positive, too. We live in a fallen world. We all have both physical and character flaws. God created man and woman to complement each other, not compete. Practicing grace and love dissolves a lot of psychological stress in our lives. It also swallows or makes us overlook many of these flaws. Showing mercy tends to release a lot of psychological tension, hence boosting your happiness.

Just expressing gratitude increases your sense of self-worth and helps you cope with stress better. Because gratitude is incompatible with negative emotions, it can diminish anger. It keeps us from taking the good things for granted.

Being gracious is a dimension of positive thinking. Choosing to be gracious, loving, appreciative, and thankful always is choosing good health. Say "thank you" as many times a day as you can. Laugh and smile all the time. This initiates a positive wave of energy that moves your momentum forward and draws you into the creative frequency of the universe. Humans are simply a bunch of energy, according to quantum physicists. That's how you generate excitement and enthusiasm. It gives you the eager look of poise and confidence. It makes your communication slick. It puts a spring in your step as you become more faithful and hopeful about life. You begin to believe more in yourself. It becomes easier to take a leap of faith into the unknown because everything begins to look like it's all vanity. Success or failure in a venture does not matter. You start to loosen the grip on your affairs. You begin to give others the benefit of the doubt. You start to be real and see the world for what it is, vanity. You realize that what goes around comes around and the best route to helping yourself is to help others. That gratitude is the best quality to put you onto the path to success. It links you with the creative universal intelligence. Call it God, nature, or whatever.

The significance is that Jesus paid the full price for us. We can walk in freedom and live eternally because Jesus set us free. He paid the full price. All you need is ask in God's spirit with belief. That is how you keep the spiritual door open for your life. In that way, you can walk in the divine spirit and watch miracles happen in your life. When God is not part of the equation for your life, it's like playing a game, leaving half of the cards off the table.

God uses us as vessels, so the Bible says. He does a lot through us. We sometimes really don't see it. He gives always in very creative ways that you may not know. Your mental fortitude, spiritual maturity, and good health are all forms of capital. Oscar, my great coach, tells me all the time that you smile to keep yourself happy, not because you are happy.

When I have a problem or feel a little discouraged, I journal gratitude. I write down a minimum of twenty-five things, sometimes many more, for which I am grateful. Thank you for the sun coming through the window. Thank you for my health, a loving family, food to eat, a place to sleep, my friends, and the sunshine. And the list goes on and on. I usually elaborate when I journal, but, even when I don't, I start each sentence by saying, "Thank you for ..." It is amazing how it is hard to stop once you start and how amazingly good I feel when I have finished. It is a very simple exercise, but one that really works. It makes you really think about everything we do have that we should be thankful for. By writing them down, it also helps to quell the negative thoughts.

What a privilege to be able to give substantial help to people. It is a real blessing for you and personally uplifting to be able to give generously. Until you have learned to give, you have not fully understood the gospel. You love because God loves you. You forgive because God forgives you. You give because he has given to you.

You may strive for worldly possessions, but, once you receive the gift of salvation, you realize that your life does not consist of material abundance. Spiritual abundance is very powerful because it sets the tone for the physical aspects of your life, that is, what you do.

When you understand the value of eternal things, you can let go of those temporal things we hold so precious. Loosen your grip on the earthly things. In the end of this life, only our spirituality will count. Imagine the wonderful feeling and peace of mind that you would have knowing that you have left the world a better place at the end of your life.

I was born in Cameroon, West Africa. I have witnessed lots of poverty firsthand. If you know the signs of poverty, you know it when you see them. I have seen somebody die in a hospital because his family did not have ten dollars for an IV fluid to save him. The hospital policy says that, when they are out of medicine because there is only so many to go around, the patient buys. During my medical training, we try to put our hands in our very shallow pockets to help such people, but, again, there is so much need, and you can only do so much. The point is, when you witness someone die because his or her family lacks ten dollars to save his or her life, it revolutionizes how you think and act.

I come from a very modest background, and I have seen much poverty, far more than the average Canadian of my age. My heart always goes out to families struggling to make ends meet.

Part of my success is to try to make a difference in the lives of poor people in the whole world. This motivated the creation of a service organization. Our mission is global poverty relief. We help people harness modern and creative methods to fight poverty. Our focus is helping people help themselves by providing them with resources they need to improve their own lives. We are dedicated to helping the hungry and homeless. We are also involved with micro-financing, disaster relief, food programs, building wells, schools, and health programs. We intend to partner with organizations that do some of the services, like Opportunity International, the Bill & Melinda Gates Foundation for eradication of malaria in Africa, and Oprah Winfrey's philanthropic work in Africa.

When I started Equity Bank Cameroon, the motivation was the same, to break the cycle of poverty. This could be done by giving loans to the poor. In that way, they can provide the basic needs of food, shelter, health care, and schooling. By helping a family to increase their income, an immediate and lasting impact on their quality of life occurs.

As business expands, the effect spreads beyond the family into the community through employment and contribution, not only locally but globally. Therefore, in order to break the cycle of poverty, you have to create a loop between the poor and financial mainstream. Capital is recycled through this loop, which benefits the poor because it enables them to get into the financial mainstream.

Although the investment vehicles used to create the loop are primarily aimed at helping the poor, the rich also benefit. The loop creates a symbiosis between the rich and poor that inevitably stokes genuine economic growth, capitalism.

That is the basis on which I coined the term *loop theory*. We end up with people who have a higher purchasing power potential for a market rather than have the poor of the poor, who are totally polarized financially.

Recycling capital is an efficient way of creating a global economic melting pot. It's a great equalizer of the market forces between the poor and the rich. Demand and supply alone are not enough to stabilize the markets. This sort of initiative, either at a personal or institutional level, fosters equity and distribution of wealth. This model has widespread applications at any level, either locally or abroad. It's an opportunity to help the hardworking poor get on the gravy train.

North America is blessed with the influx of capital from all over the world. What a privilege to enjoy the benefits of so much capital, some of which we did not create, such as musical, cultural, medical, and spiritual gifts. Be a great contributor of the global economic melting pot with the highest calling, service. Gratitude is everything, including appreciation, giving, forgiveness, nonjudgment, caring, generosity, thanksgiving, service, happiness, and loving.

Becoming the Success Master

Nimble Jack confided in Dr. Molly after he became one of the top executives in his organization. He said the world is full of dreamers, people who can sing the same song as you, but lack the action habit. Nimble Jack started getting his big breaks when he started believing in himself and putting what he believed into practice. Achievement comes from learning and practicing the simple, basic things that are common knowledge to most people. Being aware of the fact that progressive, consistent, small steps every day can produce miracles in your life is important.

Believing in yourself is very powerful because it tells you the level of self-respect that you think you deserve. The images of what you want to be come out of there. It determines what you stand for on a personal level and on your worldview as well. Whether you know it or not, most of the time, you are accountable for either your success or failure. The external factors only count for 20 percent of the solutions to your problems.

Nimble Jack's strategy for success was very simple. Yet it dramatically improved both his personal and professional lives. One of the things he did was initiate a project to create a new product for his company. As you think about it, isn't that what leading is all about? Whether for yourself or others, you want to move on to something better.

He acted upon this by getting out of bed early each day and working on his dream. He decided he was going to live his life by design, not default. He took his dream to bed with him every night. He visualized before falling asleep. This honed the dream in on his subconscious mind and made him stay focused on where he was going.

He implanted the heroic mission into his mind every day. He told me that keeping his heroic mission like a mirror every day made him more energized and cemented it into his mind.

Jack's great motivator for growth came after he separated from his wife. He started paying the mortgage alone, so he decided to develop a new product line as a way to increase productivity. So the pressure was on. He had no choice. He made use of a crisis situation. Rather than worry about the separation from his wife, he decided to turn the situation into something positive. Jack learned not to allow the negative impact his heroic mission.

As a leader, you should be aware that challenges will always come. Be ready to stay relaxed and expect the best. You have the power within you to create whatever you want. So learn to become a self-made man. Surveys show that most great leaders are self-made. They view obstacles as opportunities. They know that difficulties produce character, which produces hope, which is very powerful. It determines your internal dialogue, and the nature of our internal dialogue dictates our success or failure. Desire also breeds hope.

Hope, like optimism, is to expect the best. It's a good use of the imagination. Worry is a poor use of imagination because you expect the worst. This attitude of mind is important because it moves your energy to the positive side of the energy scale. It makes you focus more on the future rather than the past. It makes you count your blessings rather than your losses. It makes you see possibilities, not limitations. It makes you feel more secure and confident rather than getting into the vicious cycle of brooding, which leads you into procrastination.

Instead, you want to be decisive. Develop the action habit by simply acting on the brilliant ideas. When you make the commitment to do it, start step one immediately. It gets you engaged into the process, so you begin to feel like there is no turning back. If you really want to write a book, the best time to start is now. Even if you do not know all of the material, go out and conduct a survey. Interview people who are adept in the area you want to write about. The possibilities are endless. Use the techniques of brainstorming discussed in chapter three.

A little action interspersed with a little thought every day is more powerful than waiting for a giant step years down the road. You have heard the expression that a journey of a thousand miles begins with one step. This is a simple but powerful concept.

Waiting to know everything before you start acting on your dream is inefficient. Good leaders are neither perfectionists nor procrastinators. They are decisive. They think about a brilliant idea. They act now, not tomorrow. If the idea works, that would be perfect. However, if it doesn't work, then it should also be no problem. The reason is simple. There is tomorrow. A good leader will try again. It's not how many times you are knocked down. It's how quickly you stand back up again.

Winners take calculated risks. It means you study the downside and make sure you can accept it if things go sour. Winners are not afraid to lose. If they lose, it energizes them. They are aware of the fact that you sometimes fail. The key is not to dwell on it because it saps your energy. Keep going. Create other big goals that energize you. These goals will make you more creative as they stimulate you. Tough-minded leaders know that life has both good and bad. They know that bad things even happen to good people. So they do not wallow in self-pity. They simply move on. Hope keeps you going all the time, especially in tough times because you expect the best. Low achievers or mediocre people give up. They play to lose rather than play to win. When you are not afraid of losing, you can afford to take calculated risk and go out of your comfort zone. This comes with high self-esteem, that is, when you are not afraid of ridicule from others, especially negative people or critics.

Nimble Jack had a plan for personal growth. This is why he sought help as part of his long-term plan for self-improvement when he was having difficulty coping in his life. Like many great leaders, he came from a very humble background. He was not born into success, but he planned to succeed. Opportunity meets the prepared mind. A constant review, day to day, reminds you of what you are up against. It keeps your vision clear in mind. For everything we do in life, the only two reasons for anything are the pursuit of pleasure or avoidance of pain. For high achievers, they use oppositional thinking to fill up their mind with the pleasure of achieving their goal. Nimble Jack's personal life significantly improved. The benefits spread to his professional life, too. He groomed himself to become one of the top executives in his company.

Faith is a great hope and confidence-builder. Your thinking pattern determines whether you move forward or not. Strive at bringing out the best from yourself or others. Believing in yourself and focusing on your action habit will easily put you at the top. On your way to the top, always remember that it's not how many times you get knocked down. It's how quickly you get back up. In the end, being a doer is crucial because nothing happens if you think all day long but don't act.

Chapter Eleven

Words to Ponder

- **Accountability:** Acknowledges and assumes responsibility for actions and decisions. Agrees to explain and be answerable for the resulting consequences of actions and decisions. Holds self and others accountable for rules and responsibilities. Can be relied upon to ensure that projects within areas of specific responsibility are completed in a timely manner. Monitors and evaluates plans, focuses on results, and measures attainment of outcomes.

- **Ambition:** A desire for the attainment of something greater. Goal-oriented. Similar to being motivated toward reaching a goal, although not necessarily tied to a single goal. The inner drive that pushes one to achieve. To aspire to something greater.

- **Analytical:** The ability to visualize, articulate, and solve complex problems and concepts and make decisions that make sense based on available information.

- **Assertiveness:** Makes decisions confidently. Is self-assured, positive, aggressive, and dogmatic. Leaders are characterized by their firmness and strength of purpose. They know what they want and need and go about achieving it assertively. They are never daunted by the challenges that they have to overcome on the path to achieving their goals.

- **Attitude:** How one carry himself or herself. A disposition or state of mind. Body language.

- **Commitment/Dedication:** Being bound to a course of action or another person(s). Has the drive **to follow through on** promises or agreement made.

Dedication means spending whatever time and energy on a task is required to get the job done rather than giving it whatever time one has available. The work of most leadership positions is not something to do if there is time. It means giving one's whole self to the task, dedicating oneself to success and leading others with him or her.

- **Creativity:** The generation of new ideas, concepts, or associations between existing ideas or concepts. How flexibly and imaginatively people approach problems. The ability to create or invent something original. The ability to transcend traditional ideas and create meaningful, new ideas. Looks for more than one great solution for any problem. Improves a process or procedure that is inefficient or outdated. Starts a brainstorming session with one's most ridiculous ideas. Thinks differently. Being able to get outside the box and take a new and different viewpoint on things. For a leader to be able to see a new future toward which he or she will lead his or her followers, creativity provides the ability to think differently and see things that others have not seen, thus giving reasons for followers to follow.

- **Decisiveness:** The perceived ability to make a clear decision. Resists outside influences and makes a decision with confidence. Does not necessarily mean making quick decisions, but makes a decision confidently based on the information available. Does not delay or avoid decision-making. When a leader makes a decision, it will be consistent and logically supportive of business priorities and core values. Exercises good judgment by making sound and well-informed decisions. Perceives the impact and implications of decisions. Makes effective and timely decisions, even when data is limited or solutions produce unpleasant consequences. Is proactive and achievement-oriented.

- **Delegation:** Gives someone else one of his or her job tasks, but maintains control and responsibility. We delegate work not to just relieve our workload, but to allow our employees we supervise to grow professionally. The old viewpoint is, "If you want something done right, do it yourself." Be clear about the delegated task. Gives employee(s) an opportunity to ask questions. Monitors progress and offers assistance as needed. Uses effective delegation to benefit both oneself and the delegate.

- **Diplomacy:** Skills in managing negotiations, handling people, and so forth so there is little or no ill will. Tact and subtle skill in dealing with people. Exercises tact or courtesy. Uses discussion to avoid hard feelings, fights, or arguments.

- **Dynamic:** Able to change and to adapt. Characterized by energy or effective action.

- **Emotional Intelligence:** The first component, self-awareness, is the ability to recognize and understand one's moods, emotions, and drives and, in particular, the impact these have on those around a person and the work environment. The second skill is self-regulation. This refers to the ability to manage one's potentially disruptive emotions and impulses effectively in order to remain composed during challenging moments and be able to think clearly and remain focused under pressure.

- **Empathy:** Capacity to understand another person's point of view or the result of such understanding. Shows fair treatment to all people. Prejudice is the enemy of justice. Displays empathy by being sensitive to the feelings, values, interests, and well-being of others.

- **Energy:** Positive attitude. Powerful in action or effect. Possesses or exhibits energy.

- **Enthusiasm:** Shows significant and genuine interest. A lively interest in a goal or pursuit. An occupation, activity, or pursuit in which such interest is shown.

- **Entrepreneurial:** Identifies opportunities to develop and market new products and services within or outside of the organization. Is willing to take risks and initiate actions that involve a deliberate risk to achieve a recognized benefit or advantage. Demonstrates initiative, the drive to make something succeed. May include assuming much of the associated risk.

- **Ethical:** Pertains to right and wrong in conduct. Morally approvable. Conforms to a standard of right behavior. Sanctioned by or operative on one's conscience or ethical judgment. Is in accordance with the rules or standards for right conduct or practice, especially the standards of a profession.

- **Excellence:** Possesses good qualities in an eminent degree. An excellent or valuable quality. That by which anyone excels.

- **Friendliness:** Generally warm, approachable, and easy to relate with in character. Encourages open communication. Encourages others to seek one out for advice or information.

- **Flexible:** Responsive to change. Adaptable. Is open to change and new information. Adapts behavior and work methods in response to new information, changing conditions, or unexpected obstacles. Adjusts rapidly to new situations warranting attention and resolution. Associates with people who encourage one to try new things. Seeks experience in new, complex situations in or our outside of the workplace. Keeps a journal to record observations on how one reacted to unexpected obstacles that were encountered on a project at work or home. Identifies and notes what could have been done differently to demonstrate more flexibility.

- **Honesty:** Is upright, fair, truthful, sincere, or frank. Honorable in principles, intentions, and actions. Is respectable, creditable, or humble. Has a good reputation. Is the human quality of communicating and acting truthfully related to truth as a value. This includes listening and any action in the human repertoire, as well as speaking. Superficially, simply states facts and views as best one truly believes them to be. It includes both honesty to others, oneself (see *self-deception*), and one's own motives and inner reality. At times, has the ability to cause misfortune to the person who displays it. As a leader, shows people that one us honest even when it means admitting to a mistake. Displays a key trait that people are looking for in their leaders. People will trust someone who actively displays honesty, not just as an honest individual, but as someone who is worth following. Displays sincerity, integrity, and candor in all actions.

- **Hopeful (vs. Fearful):** The feeling that what is wanted can be had or events will turn out for the best. Looks forward to something with desire and reasonable confidence. Wishes for something with the expectation of the wish being fulfilled. Believes a better or positive outcome is possible even when there is some evidence to the contrary. Leaders can be both hopeful and realistic as long as the possibilities for change remain open. Calculates the odds with an optimistic eye. Is aware of the consequences of being fateful without being preordained to the inevitability of a situation or circumstance. Attempts to understand the concrete conditions of reality. Sees one's own role in it realistically. Engages in such efforts of thoughtful action as might be expected to bring about the hoped-for change. The affect of hope, in this case, has an activating effect. It helps mobilize the energies needed for activity.

- **Humor:** The trait of appreciating (and being able to express) the humorous. An alternative or surprising shift in perception or answer is given that still shows relevance and can explain a situation. A sense of humor is part of the art of leadership, getting along with people, and getting things done. Leadership is about motivating and inspiring others, and it requires a variety of skills, including humor. It is a virtue because it positively enhances personal and organizational well-being. Even under the most frustrating work conditions, it enables leaders to return perspective to the situation, restore sanity and fraying tempers, and keep people going when all they want to do is quit. In organizational terms, humor allows leaders to increase morale and productivity, drive corporate culture, and strengthen alignment. Laughter is a powerful way to reduce tension and stress, create a sense of well-being, increase contentment and alertness, and help us to place the problems and difficulties of life in context. Humor is a means of communication.

- **Innovative:** Develops new insights into situations and applies innovative solutions to make organizational improvements. Creates a work environment that encourages creative thinking and innovation. Designs and implements new or cutting-edge programs and processes. Looks for more than one great solution for any problem. Improves a process or procedure that is inefficient or outdated. Makes timely and appropriate changes in thinking, plans, and methods. Shows creativity by thinking of new and better goals, ideas, and solutions to problems.

- **Insight:** Apprehends the true nature of a thing, especially through intuitive understanding. Sees into inner character or underlying truth. Understands the relationships that sheds light on or helps solve a problem. Understands the motivational forces behind one's actions, thoughts, or behavior. The power of acute observation and deduction, discernment, perception, or introspection.

- **Inspiration:** To stimulate to action. To motivate others toward a specific goal. Passion, purpose, listening, and meaning help make a leader inspirational. Important to inspiration is the integrity of the person leading. Inclusion goes beyond the listening and feedback. For real inclusion, people need to feel intimately connected to the actions and process that are leading to the accomplishment of the goals or the decision. Displays confidence in all that one does. By showing endurance in mental, physical, and spiritual stamina, one will inspire others to reach for new heights. Takes charge when necessary.

- **Integrity:** Instills mutual trust and confidence. Creates a culture that fosters high standards of ethics. Behaves in a fair and ethical manner toward others. Demonstrates a sense of corporate responsibility and commitment to public service. Questions one's work decisions. Determines if they reflect the values and values of the organization. When in conflict, explores alternatives. Aligns words and actions with inner values. Sticks to these values even when an alternative path may be easier or more advantageous. A leader with integrity can be trusted and will be admired for sticking to strong values. He or she also acts as a powerful model for people to copy, thus building an entire organization with powerful and effective cultural values.

- **Knowledge:** Knows the facts, truths, or principles. Understands oneself and one's character and abilities. The perception of fact or truth. Clear and certain mental apprehension. Is well-informed, which is critical in the decision-making process. Expertise and skills acquired by a person through experience or education. The theoretical or practical understanding of a subject or branch of learning. The confident understanding of a subject with the ability to use it for a specific purpose if appropriate. Success in leadership depends also on the degree of the knowledge, understanding, and appreciation of the needs and expectations of those who are to be led and of how the group is structured, especially as to the relevant situation immediately confronting them in their environment.

- **Legacy:** To leave a lasting impression. The type of leadership one consistently exhibits will affect one's legacy. Communication is essential in shaping a leadership legacy. If a leader has a strong vision and a sense of direction, others will stay on for the duration and work diligently toward the objective, even if the leader is no longer present or has moved on. To leave a legacy, a leader must be a visionary, looking beyond today's actions to how the actions will affect the future.

- **Loyalty:** Faithful adherence to a leader and his or her vision. Unswerving in one's allegiance. Is faithful to a cause, ideal, person, or custom. To be an effective leader, followers must have trust in him or her. They need to be sold on the vision (be loyal to the leader). In any organization, a leader's actions set the pace. This behavior wins trust and loyalty and ensures the organization's continued vitality. One of the ways to build trust is to display a good sense of character composed of beliefs, values, skills, and traits.

- **Moral:** One's actions should be based on reason and moral principles. Does not make decisions based on childlike emotional desires or feelings.

- **Negotiating:** A dialogue intended to resolve disputes, produce an agreement on a course of action, bargain for individual or collective advantage, or craft outcomes to satisfy various interests. To confer with others to come to terms or reach an agreement or decision. Even before the negotiation process starts, people in a positive mood have more confidence and higher tendencies to plan to use a cooperative strategy. Positive effects of negotiation include an increased satisfaction with achieved outcome and an influence on one's desire for future interactions.

- **Networking:** A supportive system of sharing information and services among individuals and groups having a common interest. Maintains a high level of mutual communication between family, friends, associates, co-workers, and so forth.

- **Openness:** Is able to listen to ideas that are outside one's current mental models. Is able to suspend judgment until after one has heard someone else's ideas. Listens to people without trying to shut them down early, which at least demonstrates care and builds trust. Also treats other ideas as potentially better than one's own ideas. In the uncertain world of new territory, the ability to openly consider alternatives is an important skill.

- **Optimistic:** Takes a favorable view of events or conditions and expects the most favorable outcome. Tends to expect the best possible outcome or dwell on the most hopeful aspects of a situation. An outlook on life such that one maintains a view of the world as a positive place. People would say that optimism is seeing the glass half-full of water as opposed to half-empty. Personal optimism correlates strongly with self-esteem, psychological well-being, and physical and mental health. Allows one to see the positive aspects of any situation. Enables one to capitalize on each possibility. Some research exists that demonstrates that optimism results in higher achievement. An optimistic belief in one and one's capabilities to positively impact situations, even ones that appear negative, fuels success.

- **Organization:** The ability to coordinate or carry out widespread activities. Effective organizational skills help lead a balanced life, cope with the competitive world, and prove oneself while still maintaining reduced stress levels.

- **Passion:** A strong or extravagant fondness, enthusiasm, or desire for anything. A powerful or compelling emotion or feeling. Applies to lively or eager interest in or admiration for a proposal, cause, or activity. Provides an individual with the light of leadership. Creates an undeniable drive to make a difference.

- **Patience:** To be quiet and have steady perseverance and diligence. To endure difficult circumstances. Is steadfast. The willingness or ability to accept conditions that do not conform to one's ideal. All leaders need to recognize how important patience can be when faced with the inevitable challenges, frustrations, and problems embedded in leading others.

- **Perceptive:** Has or shows keenness of insight, understanding, or intuition. We gather information about the world and interact with it through our actions. Perceptual information is critical for action. The capacity for comprehension, quick, acute, and intuitive cognition. Fully understand the decision one must make along with all of the facts and information involved in the situation one must resolve.

- **Persistence:** Continues despite opposition, obstacles, discouragement, and so forth. Perseveres. A will to win or reach one's goal. Driving force to achieve and push others to achieve.

- **Prioritize:** The ability to organize or deal situations according to their level of importance in the situation at hand. Leaders must prioritize tasks in order to manage their time effectively.

- **Proactive:** The ability to act before a situation becomes a source of confrontation or crisis. The exceptional leader is always thinking three steps ahead. Works to master his or her own environment with the goal of avoiding problems before they arise.

- **Problem-solving:** Identifies and analyzes problems. Distinguishes between relevant and irrelevant information to make logical decisions. Provides solutions to individual and organizational problems. Always considers ideas and opinions of others. Two minds work better than one. Seeks out complex tasks or projects.

- **Professional:** Adheres to standards of practice. Has professional character, spirit, or methods. Defined by how well one interact with everyone, including peers, supervisors, staff, and so forth. The active demonstration of the traits of a professional (knowledge and skills of the profession, commitment to self-improvement of skills and knowledge, service orientation, pride in the profession, covenantal relationship with client, creativity and innovation, conscience and trustworthiness, accountability for his or her work, ethically sound decision-making, and leadership).

- **Rational:** To understand reason and be sensible. Has or exercises sound judgment or good sense. Includes "uncertain but sensible" arguments based on probability, expectation, personal experience, and the like, whereas logic deals principally with provable facts and demonstrably valid relations between them.

- **Resourcefulness:** The ability to deal skillfully and promptly with new situations, difficulties, and so forth. Can devise ways and means to solve problems. Utilizes the resources available to one. A leader must create access to information. Leaders fill operational gaps by moving people, resources, and ideas into the right direction.

- **Responsibility:** Is answerable or accountable, as for something within one's power, control, or management. Has a capacity for moral decisions and therefore accountable. Able to answer for one's conduct and obligations. Accepts responsibility for one's actions and those of the team, sending a loud message to others.

Global Leadership

You can support any of these initiatives by Dr. Nkut:

The Nkut Foundation
2956 Hwy 69 N Unit #2
Val Caron, Ontario
P3N 1E3
Toll-free: (888) 333-7854
Tel: (705) 919-3349
Fax: (705) 897-2344
Web site: www.nkutfoundation.com
Mission: Fighting poverty, globally and locally
Focus: Raising money for poverty relief projects

Skylimit Corporation
1877 Paris Street
Sudbury, Ontario
P3E 3C5
Tel: (705) 523-3336
Fax: (705) 523-5554
Mission: Serving the financially needy
Focus: Payday loans

Equity Bank Cameroon
Immeuble Pharmacie Bell
Douala, Cameroon
B.P. 4876 Douala
Tel: (237) 3342-6479
Fax: (237) 3343-2634
Mission: Create abundance to relieve poverty
Focus: Recycle capital (loop theory) and micro-financing.

About the Author

Dr. Alfred Nkut, M.D., is an accomplished physician, entrepreneur, and philanthropist with avid interest in leadership. His experience has shown him that self-improvement, especially development of character goals, is not emphasized in most formal educational systems. For this reason, he grew increasingly interested in studying, learning, growing, and researching to provide additional insight into the subject of leadership.

Dr. Nkut sees every day as an opportunity to add value not only to his own life, but to the lives of others as well. This is emphasized by the fact that his practice of family medicine is complimented by the establishment of a foundation – The Nkut Foundation – whose mission is to harness modern and creative methods to fight poverty. He has also founded the Skylimit Corporation to make a difference in the lives of people, and a financial institution in Cameroon, West Africa with the goal of poverty relief.

The more he learns and understands the area of leadership and success, the more passion he has for sharing that knowledge and for encouraging those who wish to improve their lives. He knows of no better way to get a kick out of life than to give, because for him giving is receiving; it is love—and that's how you make your way to "heaven."

Dr. Nkut and his wife, Dr. Elaine Blacklock, both practice medicine in Greater Sudbury, Ontario, Canada, and are proud to call the city home along with their children Jacob and Ruthie.

LaVergne, TN USA
19 July 2010
190047LV00001B